THE EARLY PIONEERS OF STEAM

THE EARLY PIONEERS OF STEAM

THE INSPIRATION BEHIND GEORGE STEPHENSON

STUART HYLTON

The
History
Press

First published 2019

The History Press
97 St George's Place, Cheltenham,
Gloucestershire, GL 50 3QB
www.thehistorypress.co.uk

British Library Cataloguing in Publication Data.
A catalogue record for this book is available from the British Library.

ISBN 978 0 7509 9128 5

Typesetting and origination by The History Press
Printed and bound in Great Britain by TJ International Ltd

Contents

Introduction   7

1   The First Steam 'Engines'   11
2   Steam Locomotion   28
3   Some Pioneers   83
4   Rainhill   99
5   Some Early Railways   116
6   Some Lessons from Canal Mania   133
7   Tracks and Tramways   144
8   The Role of Parliament   163
9   Railways and the Industrial Revolution   177
10 Supplier of Railways to the World   191

Sources   217
Bibliography   218
Index   221

Cover image: A view back into railway history. Lyon, a Hetton Colliery locomotive, originally dating from 1822 but now thought to have been built in 1851–52 as a replica of an 1822 locomotive designed by Nicholas Wood (1795–1865). Wood was a close associate of George Stephenson (Stephenson's son Robert was apprenticed to Wood). It was photographed for *Railway Magazine* in 1905 and remained in service until 1912. In 1925 the locomotive took part – under its own steam – in the centenary celebrations of the Stockton and Darlington Railway. It was one of a pair (the other was destroyed by a boiler explosion in 1858/9). (Mary Evans Picture Library)

A first-class carriage from the earliest days of the Liverpool and Manchester Railway.

Introduction

The opening of the Liverpool and Manchester Railway on 15th September 1830 was one of the epochal moments which 'divide precisely the past from the future, the old from the new, the historic from the prehistoric and of which nothing that came after was ever quite the same as anything gone before'.

Sir Arthur Elton, quoted in Gwyn and Cossons

In 1832 an essay on the advantages of railways compared road travel and rail travel between Liverpool and Manchester before and after the opening of the railway. By road, the journey took four hours and cost ten shillings inside the coach and five shillings outside. By train the same journey took one and three quarter hours and cost five shillings inside and three shillings and sixpence outside. Compared to canal the time savings were even more significant. The same journey had taken twenty hours by canal. The cost of canal carriage was fifteen shillings a ton, whereas by rail it was ten shillings a ton.

www.parliament.uk

The great work of the Liverpool and Manchester Railway, advancing towards completion, seemed by a common unanimity of opinion, to be deemed as <u>the</u> experiment which was to decide the fate of Rail-ways. The eyes of the whole scientific world were upon that great undertaking; public opinion on the subject remained suspended; and hence its progress was watched with the most intense interest.

Nicholas Wood, A Practical Treatise on Rail Roads, 1832

Many of the general public think of the Stephensons and Brunel as the fathers of the railways, and their Liverpool and Manchester and Great Western Railways as the prototypes of the modern systems. But who were the railways' grandfathers and great grandfathers? For the rapid evolution of the railways after 1830 depended to a considerable degree upon the Stephensons, Brunel and their contemporaries being able to draw upon lifetimes of experience in using and developing railways, and of harnessing the power of steam. Giants the Stephensons and Brunel may have been, but they stood upon the shoulders of many other considerable – if lesser-known – talents.

The purpose of this book is to recognise the many great contributions made over the centuries, leading to the eventual emergence of the steam railways. Among the things it looks at are:

- the use of steam power to generate movement – a story going back to the time of the ancient Egyptians;
- the use of railways to serve industry and transport, which can be dated back at least to the first millennium BC and the ancient Greek Diolkos;
- British Parliamentary processes being used to facilitate (or control) the building of railways, first recorded in 1758. This had a marked effect on the form railway building took in Britain;
- The earlier transport revolution of the canals, involving the creation of massive civil engineering works and the assembly of equally massive streams of finance to build them, which would later be needed to fund the explosive growth of the railway network;
- The emergence of the Industrial Revolution, which could not have happened in the form it did without a means for the swift mass movement of people and goods;
- The stories of some of the individuals who made a mark in the earliest days of the railway, the railways they built and ran and the locomotives they designed;
- How British steam railway technology was spread throughout the world and helped to ensure the universality of this invaluable aid to modern living.

The book will look at the many people and events that influenced the dawn of the railway age. I am grateful, not only to them but also to the many people who have written about them. I have acknowledged my main published sources at the back of the book. In addition, there is a wealth of research now available on the internet, for which I am also duly grateful. My index of internet sources is less complete, since you can see what is available by entering your topic of interest into your search engine.

I have tried to avoid infringing anybody's copyright but if I have inadvertently failed in any particular instance, please let me know via the publisher and I will try to ensure that it is put right in any future editions.

Stuart Hylton

1

The First Steam 'Engines'

This book looks at not one but two developments that were of vital significance to the industrial world in which we live. Taken individually, each one was of major importance to us. Brought together, their effect on the world was transformative. Each has been known about for centuries, but it was not until the start of the nineteenth century that their combined potential began to be realised.

We begin by looking at the very earliest attempts to create steam engines of one sort or another – at first, as curiosities or toys, but gradually evolving into devices that could do useful work. But what is an engine? It is a device that converts energy into mechanical power. For our present purposes we are talking about heat engines – engines that consume fuel to make heat, which is then converted into mechanical energy. They can be subdivided into internal and external combustion. A car's petrol engine is an example of internal combustion. Petrol is injected into the engine and ignited. The hot gases this creates move the pistons that make the engine work. A steam engine, by contrast, is an external combustion engine. Fuel is burnt outside the engine, which creates heat that turns water into steam. The steam is then fed into the engine, to drive the pistons and make the engine work.

When water is turned into steam, the steam takes up about 1,600 times the space that was occupied by the water from which it was made. If it is not allowed to expand, it exerts pressure on whatever is preventing its expansion. It is this that is the driving force of all steam engines.

Hero of Alexandria's Aeolipile – the first steam engine?

The story of the steam engine begins, improbably, in first-century Alexandria, a city in Roman-occupied Egypt. One of the tutors at its centre of learning, the Musaeum, was a man named Hero (or Heron). He lived between about AD 10 and 70, taught mathematics and physics, and in some people's estimations was an inventive genius to rival Archimedes, Euclid or Pythagoras (or, to set it in a more modern context, Leonardo da Vinci or Thomas Edison). His versatile imagination foresaw (at least in theory) programmable computers, robots, vending machines and surveying instruments, but among his other inventions was the aeolipile, described in Hero's AD 60 book *Spiritulia seu Pneumatica.*

The aeolipile is also known as Hero's Engine (although Vitruvius mentions it a century before in his *De Architectura,* it is not certain that he was talking about the same thing). Hero's version has been described as a 'rocket-like reaction engine' and 'the first recorded steam engine'. It has a central water container, in which the water is boiled. The steam from it is passed into a turbine and vented through bent or curved nozzles, generating thrust and causing the turbine to rotate. In this, it anticipates the principles of rocketry and of Newton's second and third laws of motion. However, nobody at the time (almost 2,000 years before the Industrial Revolution) could see a practical application for the aeolipile (beyond a related device, for what seemed an unnecessarily complicated piece of machinery for opening temple doors). The aeolipile was to remain a 'temple wonder', or object of reverence with no serious function, for centuries to come.

The aeolipile idea was revisited in the seventeenth century by the Italian engineer **Giovanni Branca** (1571–1645) in his book *Le Machine* (1629). It was suggested that his 'steam engine' could drive a variety of applications, but it proved to be a blind alley, and not much of an advance over what Hero had proposed centuries before.

It was further revived in the nineteenth century, when railway pioneer **Richard Trevithick** tried building a giant version of the aeolipile. This was essentially a boiler feeding steam to a Catherine wheel up to 24ft (7.3m) in diameter, with steam jets coming off it. Trevithick worked on it until his death, but could not get it to build up a sufficient head of steam to work efficiently, and the idea finally had to be abandoned.

The idea of an aeolipile is sometimes said to have been quoted in 1680, in **Isaac Newton**'s *Explanations of the Newtonian Philosophy*, in which he was supposed to have included a drawing of a vehicle propelled by a jet of steam. This is apparently untrue. The idea actually appeared in a book on Newtonian philosophy by Willem 's Gravesande (1720), and was given only as a theoretical illustration of one of Newton's laws, rather than being proposed as a practicable proposition with applications.

By complete contrast, there was a report from France in 1125 of a church organ that was worked by air escaping from a vessel in which it had been compressed 'by heated water'.

In the sixteenth century a Turkish polymath named **Taqi ad-Din Muhammad ibn Ma'ruf** (1526–85) was working in Istanbul. He wrote more than ninety books on a variety of subjects, but among his claims to fame was the invention of a self-rotating spit that was an early stage in the history of the steam turbine. It used steam to turn the vanes, which in turn rotated the axle at the end of the spit. Again, it had no great impact, either on modes of transport or the barbecue industry.

The size and weight of atmospheric steam engines was a major impediment to their use in any means of transport. But size and weight were slightly less critical in ships, which may be why ideas for steam-powered boats appeared somewhat before the equivalent land vehicles. Possibly the earliest contender for the title of inventor of the steamboat was **Blasco de Garay,** though his claim was by no means uncontested. De Garay (1500–52) was a Spanish naval captain at the time of the Holy Roman Emperor Charles V, and also a prolific inventor. He submitted a series of naval-related inventions to Charles V, including diving apparatus and the use of paddle wheels as a substitute for oars, as well as a steam-powered ship.

Details of this did not emerge until 1825, when Tomas Gonzalez, Director of the Royal Archives of Simancas, came across details in a file that he had found. These were then published in 1826 by the sailor and historian Martin Fernandez Navarrete. Part of Gonzalez' letter to Navarette reads as follows:

> Blasco de Garay, a captain in the navy, proposed in 1543, to the Emperor and King, Charles V, a machine to propel large boats and ships, even in calm weather, without oars or sails. In spite of the impediments and the opposition that this project met with, the Emperor ordered a trial to be made of it in the port of Barcelona, which in fact took place on the 17th on the month of June of the said year 1543. Garay would not explain the particulars of his discovery; it was evident however during the experiment that it consisted in a large kettle of boiling water, and in moving wheels attached to each side of the ship. The experiment was tried on a ship of two hundred tons, called the Trinidad, which came from Colibre to discharge a cargo of corn at Barcelona, of which Peter de Scarza was captain. By order of Charles V, Don Henry de Toledo the governor, Don Pedro de Cordova the treasurer Ravago, and the vice-chancellor, and intendant of Catalonia witnessed the experiment. In the reports made to the Emperor and to the prince, this ingenious invention was generally approved, particularly on account of the promptness and facility with which the ship was made to go about. [...] The Emperor promoted the inventor one grade, made him a present of two hundred thousand maravedis (maravedi – a medieval Spanish copper coin) and ordered the expense to be paid out of the Treasury.

Given the distinguished list of alleged witnesses to this event, it is surprising that it should have vanished into obscurity for almost three centuries. But the Spanish authorities subsequently discredited the account and the first 'official' steamboat to enter Spanish waters was the *Real Fernando* in 1817.

A Spaniard, Jeronimo de Ayanz y Beaumont, was granted a patent in 1606 for a steam-powered water pump that managed to drain some mines.

The French-born physicist **Denis Papin** (of whom, more shortly) also built the first piston steam engine, which he used to power a boat in 1707. His plan was to bring it from the River Weser to England, for trials on the Thames. But the boatmen on the Weser, fearing for their livelihoods, seized and destroyed it. But Dendy Marshall suggests that this boat was only a model; that the full-sized boat Papin produced was reliant on man-power and was only intended to have been driven by steam later on, if such a thing proved to be possible. It was left to Scotsman William Symington, with his *Charlotte Dundas* of 1802, to produce the world's first practicable full-sized steamboat.

For the next advance in steam-powered motion we turn to a Flemish Jesuit priest, Father **Ferdinand Verbiest** (1623–88), who was a missionary to seventeenth-century China. His main claims to fame were as a diplomat, cartographer and translator. However, in around 1672 he also designed a steam-powered trolley as a toy for the Chinese Emperor, quite possibly the first steam-powered vehicle. Verbiest describes it in his *Astronomia Europea*. It consisted of a ball-shaped boiler from which the steam was directed onto a simple open 'steam turbine' (rather like a water wheel) that drove the rear wheels. Two doubts surround this being counted as a major development in steam transport. First, it was only just over 2ft long, and as such not able to carry a payload, let alone a human driver. Second, there was no evidence that the drawings ever got built and tested.

By the early eighteenth century a much more concerted effort was being made to harness the power of steam for industry, (albeit not necessarily for the purpose of transport) and a number of notable thinkers devoted their time to it.

Working Engines

Thomas Savery (*c.*1650–1715) was a Devon-born military engineer who spent his spare time conducting experiments in mechanics. Among his earlier experiments was a device for rowing becalmed ships, involving paddle wheels powered by a capstan (which the Royal Navy declined to take up). In July 1698 he patented the first commercially used steam engine, which the patent described as:

A new invention for the raising of water and occasioning motion to all
sorts of mill work by the impellent force of fire, which will be of great use
and advantage for draining mines, serving towns with water, and for the
working of all sorts of mills where they have not the benefit of water nor
constant winds.

Weightman describes it more prosaically as 'a fairly simple contraption in
which steam was run into a cylinder, where it was cooled with cold water,
causing a vacuum, which sucked the water up from a mine and spewed it
out'. The terms of his patent implied that Savery's machine was a multi-
purpose engine, but this was not the case. All it was really good for was
pumping water, and even that not very efficiently.

Savery demonstrated the machine to the Royal Society in June 1699, but
his patent itself was very vaguely drawn, having neither illustrations nor even a
description of how it worked. The first such description appeared in Savery's

1702 book *The Miner's Friend; or, an
Engine to Raise Water by Fire* (in which
he at least explained the claim that it
could be used to pump water out of
mines). How true was this in practice?
We will look at the Savery machine's
working in a little more detail.

Savery's engine had no piston; the only
moving parts were the taps. Steam was
raised in the boiler and admitted into one
of the first working vessels. It would blow
out through a downpipe into the water
that was being raised. Once the system
was hot and full of steam, the tap between
the boiler and the working vessel was

Thomas Savery, inventor of the first
steam mine pump.

shut and (if necessary) the vessel was cooled down. This made the steam inside
it condense back into water, creating a partial vacuum. Atmospheric pressure
would then push water up the downpipe until the vessel was full. The tap below
the vessel would then be closed and the tap between it and the up-pipe opened,
and more steam was admitted from the boiler. As the steam pressure built up, it
forced water from the vessel up the up-pipe to the top of the mine.

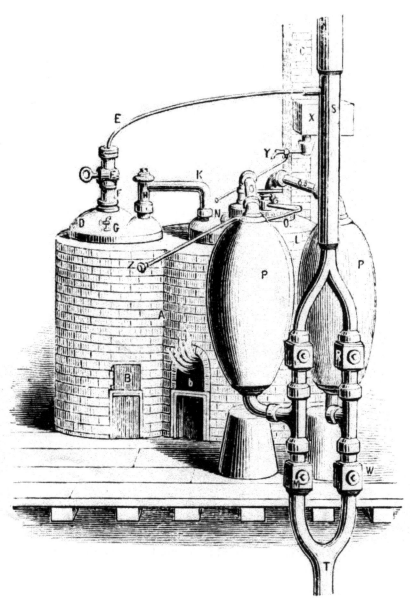

Savery's pumping engine.

This engine had major problems:

- It was very slow. When water was admitted to the working vessel, much of the heat was wasted in warming up the water that was being pumped;
- It involved relatively high-pressure steam and the technology of the day

could not cope with it. The soldered joints needed frequent repair and there was the ever-present risk of a boiler explosion. Related to this;

- To clear water from a deep mine would have needed a series of moderate pressure engines, reaching from the bottom of the mine to the top in instalments, since the technology of the day could not have coped with the pressures required for a single machine doing longer lifts of water. This would have been impracticable. As a result;

- Because only atmospheric pressure was (theoretically) used to push water up into the engine, it could not be located more than about 25ft above the water level. (The theoretical maximum under laboratory conditions was about 33ft, but this could not be achieved in real life). A further 40ft of depth could be added using steam pressure with the technology of the day, but even this would not be enough to clear a typical mine of water. Savery claimed that his engine would raise a full bore of water up 80ft 'with great ease'. But to do so, the boiler would have had to withstand a pressure of about 35psi, roughly that of a modern car tyre. This may help to explain the Savery machines' reputation for exploding;

- The primitive design of the boilers made them very inefficient and heavy on fuel, even disregarding the inefficiency of the process itself, involving constantly heating and cooling the engine;

- Finally, it was not strictly an engine as we defined it; as we saw it had no moving parts other than the taps, and no means of directly transmitting its power to any other kind of machinery (such as factory or mill machines).

The ideal solution to the problem might have been a mechanical pump at the mine's surface, which would have lifted the water out of the mine, rather than sucking it up with the aid of atmospheric pressure. Such pumps were commonplace – powered by horses – but Savery's device was not a steam-powered replacement for them, since he had no reciprocating drive to power it.

Savery's loosely worded patent covered all forms of engine that raised water using fire, and the 1698 patent's fourteen years' protection was extended by a further twenty-one years (the so-called Fire Engine Act, granted by Parliament because it had exaggerated hopes for its success). One consequence of this was that Newcomen (see later), with his more advanced steam engine, was forced to go into partnership with Savery and pay Savery royalties on each one he sold.

The Savery engine was much cheaper to buy than the Newcomen; a 2–4hp Savery engine might be had for between £150 and £200. It was also available in much smaller sizes, right down to one horsepower – much smaller than any engine Newcomen made. This was because piston steam engines were very inefficient in small sizes, right up until the twentieth century.

The experience of using Savery machines appears to have been mixed. One at York buildings in London tried to generate steam at eight to ten times the atmospheric pressure, blowing all the joints on the machine. Similar problems were encountered while trying to drain water from a pool in Staffordshire, and some nearby mines. But others, at Hampton Court and Campden House, Kensington, appear to have given reliable service, and Savery engines were produced well into the late eighteenth century.

Savery's work apparently bears a striking resemblance to something in a book of inventions published in 1663 by Edward Somerset, Marquis of Worcester. One (unproven) account has it that Savery bought up as many copies of Somerset's book as he could find and destroyed them, so as not to let it steal his thunder.

Savery ended his career as Surveyor of Waterworks at Hampton Court Palace.

Denis Papin (1647–1712) was a French Huguenot who originally studied to be a doctor, but discovered that his real interest lay in mathematics and mechanics. He secured a post working for Christiaan Huygens, one of the leading scientists of the day, where Papin worked in experiments with air pumps from 1671 to 1674. This work led to him being introduced to the English physicist Robert Boyle, with whom he also worked, before he became assistant to Robert Hooke at the Royal Society. In 1679 he demonstrated one of his inventions to the Society, a device that:

> Exemplified the enormous elastic force that steam acquires when heated and confined. The properties of this digester for cooking and extracting gelatine from bones by high pressure steam contains all that is at present practiced in the preparation of food by this method.

His 'digester' was what we would call a pressure cooker, but the path from there into steam engines is not too difficult to see. Papin returned to France in 1681 but the increasing persecution of Huguenots forced him into permanent exile in 1685.

It was in 1690 that he published his first work on the steam engine, *De novis quibusdam machinis*. It was based on the work of Thomas Savery. The purpose of this particular machine was to raise water to a canal in Germany, though he also developed a steam engine to pump water to a rooftop tank in a palace, from where it would supply water for the fountains in the grounds. He documented his ideas in *The New Art of Pumping Water by Using Steam* (1707), in which a second machine incorporated a safety valve of his own design to prevent dangerous levels of steam pressure from building up. It was needed, given the lack of understanding of the day about regulating cooking temperatures and steam pressure, whoch caused many of his experiments to crack or explode. This second engine worked off steam, rather than atmospheric, pressure.

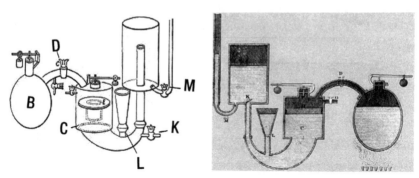

Papin's pump of 1704.

Papin's steam cylinder and piston experiment was his greatest contribution to the steam age. Water enters the pump through valve L. The boiler (B) and Cylinder (C) are fitted with weighted safety valves. When valve D is opened steam is admitted to the cylinder, forcing down the piston, pushing the water beneath it into the reservoir through valve K and in the process compressing the air above it. The steam in cylinder C is then condensed to form a vacuum, which forces the piston upwards, drawing more water into the system through valve L and closing valve K. Closing valve K removes the steam pressure, causing the water in the reservoir to be expelled through valve M under the action of the compressed air above it.

Like some of his other inventions, Papin's experiment worked, but only sufficiently to demonstrate the feasibility of the principles behind them. He did not persevere with them for long enough to develop a practical working engine. His atmospheric steam engine from 1690 was very similar to the one successfully produced by Thomas Newcomen in 1712 and his development of the first cylinder-and-piston steam engine was a vital part of the Industrial Revolution.

Papin has been described as 'a formidably obstinate character, a man incapable of conceding the least advantage to his adversary, a skilled expert in the rules and tricks of the art of disputing'.

Could this be at least part of the reason why he died in London in 1712 in obscurity and poverty, the importance of his work not recognised in his lifetime?

Thomas Newcomen (1664–1729) was born in Dartmouth, Devon, and made his living as an ironmonger, specialising in the needs of the mining industry. As such, he was keenly aware of the problem of flooding that was faced by coal and tin mines. He was also a lay preacher and a leading light of the Baptist community, with whom he had business links. This may have included the family of Thomas Savery, whose forebears were merchants in south Devon, where Newcomen originated.

The atmospheric engine, invented by him in about 1712, was the first practical machine to use steam to produce mechanical work. As we have seen, there had been various devices illustrating the principle over the years, but up until now these had either been novelties with no real practical application, or had serious design faults that prevented their being very effective for their intended purpose.

Newcomen drew upon the ideas of Thomas Savery and Denis Papin. From Savery he borrowed the idea of a 'thermic syphon', where steam is let into an empty container and then condensed to create a vacuum. This vacuum was intended to be used in Savery's model to suck water from the bottom of the mine. Following Papin, Newcomen took the idea of replacing Savery's receiving vessel (where the steam was condensed) with a cylinder and piston, where atmospheric pressure pulls down the piston.

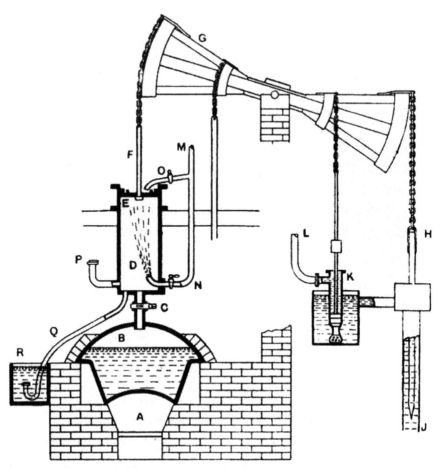

A cutaway diagram of a Newcomen atmospheric engine.

The Newcomen engine does its pumping by mechanical means. Put very simply, it had a boiler (A) located immediately beneath a cylinder (D) containing an inverted piston (E). The boiler produced quantities of low-pressure (and hence safe) steam. The cylinder is attached to one end of a heavy beam (G), pivoted at the centre. The other end of the beam is attached by a chain to a rod (H), which drives the pumping machinery down in the mine by its up-and-down movement.

The pumping equipment attached to the beam is heavier than the steam piston, so the resting position for the beam is pump side down/ engine side up – known as 'out of the house'. But we will start with the piston at the bottom of the cylinder. As the piston rises under the weight of the pumping equipment, low-pressure steam from the boiler is let into the cylinder. The steam does little of the lifting – that is done mainly by the weight of the pumping gear. Once the piston reaches the top of its stroke, the steam valve is closed and some cold water (coming from a tank at the top of the pumphouse) (M) is sprayed into the cylinder. This cools the steam, condensing it back into water and leaving a partial vacuum in the cylinder. Atmospheric pressure then presses down on the top of the piston, driving it back down the cylinder (hence the alternative name for this apparatus – atmospheric engine). At the end of the downward stroke, the cooling water is drained from the cylinder and the engine is ready to start again. This cycle is repeated about twelve times a minute.

The earlier Newcomen engines had a copper boiler which domed top (B) was made of lead, and which could withstand no more pressure than 1 to 2psi. Later ones were made of small riveted iron plates. Another sign of the primitive technology of the day was that the cylinder was finished by hand and was not always true. So the piston had to be surrounded by a flexible seal in the form of a leather or rope ring around it. But even this was not a perfect solution, and a layer of water had to be permanently maintained on the top of the piston to complete the seal.

Newcomen's machine was extremely inefficient and expensive but still a great advance on anything that had preceded it, being rugged and reliable. The first working version of the engine was installed in a coal mine in Dudley Castle in Staffordshire in 1712. Its cylinder was 21in in diameter by almost 8ft long and it ran at about twelve strokes a minute, raising 10 gallons of water from a depth of 156ft. It was rated at about 5.5hp and its efficiency at about 1 per cent. The second was in Griff Colliery, near Coventry. It replaced more than fifty horses and cut the cost of draining the mine from £900 to £150 a year.

The Newcomen engine was a great success. Until 1733, they had to be manufactured under Savery's all-embracing patent, by which time about 125 engines had been installed, both in this country and in mining areas throughout Europe. By 1775 some 600 Newcomen engines had been built. Some of these were huge machines; improved casting techniques enabled machines with cylinders of up to 6ft (1.8m) in diameter to be built by the 1760s.

Although they were a step up from their predecessors and a much greater commercial success, the problem was that the Newcomen machines were still not efficient. This may have been partly due to the limits of the engineering techniques of the day, but more fundamental was the fact that a lot of heat was lost when condensing the steam. The loss of heat had to be replaced, meaning that Newcomen engines consumed fuel at a rapid rate. They must take their share of the blame for William Blake's 'dark satanic mills', the perpetual pall of smoke that hung over Victorian industrial areas and their steam-driven mines and factories.

As we saw, this inefficiency was much less of a problem (at least financially) for coal mining users of the engine, for they had unsaleable 'small coal' on site to use as virtually free fuel. But for others, such as the Cornish tin miners, without local coal supplies, the cost of coal was a heavy burden, with it having to be imported by a combination of ship, horse and cart, and packhorse. At its worst, the cost of running a Newcomen engine could be prohibitive. According to one estimate, more than half the Newcomen engines in the West Country were lying idle by the 1770s.

James Watt

The people are steam-mill mad. The velocity, violence, magnitude and horrible noise of the engine give universal satisfaction to all beholders.

James Watt

Efforts were made over the years to improve the efficiency of the Newcomen engine. John Smeaton built many improved large engines, though he was better known as a civil engineer. But, according to some accounts, the big breakthrough came in 1763, when the University of Glasgow sent a miniature version of a Newcomen engine for repair. They entrusted it to a small workshop within the university itself, run by James Watt. Watt's business dealt with all sorts of mechanical objects – mathematical and musical instruments, toys and other goods, but steam engines were his passion.

Even after he had repaired it, (if, indeed he did – Dendy Marshall attributes the repair to a colleague, Doctor J. Robison) Watt found that it

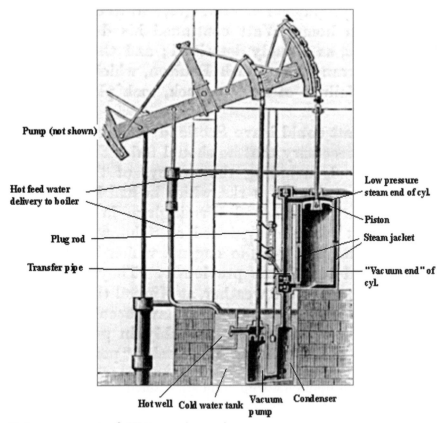

Pump (not shown)

Hot feed water delivery to boiler

Plug rod

Transfer pipe

Low pressure steam end of cyl

Piston

Steam jacket

"Vacuum end" of cyl

Hot well   Cold water tank   Vacuum pump   Condenser

Major components of a Watt pumping engine.

still hardly worked (it is a feature of Newcomen engines that the smaller the engine, the more pronounced its inefficiency will be.) Watt found that three-quarters of the energy of the steam was being wasted in reheating the cylinder after each cycle, only for it to be cooled again when cold water was injected to condense the steam.

Watt's big idea (dating from 1765) was to have a separate chamber, away from the piston, where the steam could be condensed. This meant that the cylinder and piston could be kept at the same temperature as the steam (especially when it was insulated in a steam jacket) and relatively little energy was lost. This arrangement reduced the fuel bill by between a third and a quarter compared with a standard Newcomen engine of the same size.

Watt had three problems with taking his idea further. One was finding the money to build it. Another, related to the first, was securing a patent for it. The third was finding someone who could engineer the cylinder and the piston with sufficient precision. The first two were not resolved until Watt formed a partnership with Matthew Boulton (of whom, more shortly). For eight years Watt had been forced to abandon his researches in favour of more gainful employment as a surveyor and then a civil engineer. The patent was secured, after much expenditure, in 1769, and in 1775 was extended until 1800. But Watt still lacked the capital to make it a marketable concern by himself. This and the engineering problem were again resolved by the Boulton partnership and by the technical expertise Boulton's business contacts could bring to bear on the matter.

The Boulton–Watt Partnership of 1775 came about by an unusual route. Watt's original business partner was an iron founder, and owner of the Carrick Ironworks, named Doctor John Roebuck. He ran into financial problems in 1772, owing Boulton £1,200, and gave Boulton his two-thirds share in Watt's patent in lieu of the debt. Boulton persuaded Watt to enter into a partnership with him, and they started developing and selling Watt's improved engines. Watt's work on them was already well known and Boulton's word of mouth ensured that his reputation spread rapidly.

Boulton's own interest in Watt's ideas originated from problems he had with his own Soho manufactory. This was powered by water and had outgrown the power that the river could deliver. Boulton's idea was to use steam power to lift water from below the waterwheel to above it – in effect to gain additional power by using the same water through the waterwheel twice.

Boulton & Watt developed an unusual method of payment for the engines. They compared the cost of running Watt's machine with that of the customer's earlier, less efficient, model and made an annual charge equivalent to one-third of the saving each year, for the next twenty-five years. This arrangement was not universally popular with the customers, though it did not stop them buying the machines – about 450 were sold between the start of the partnership in 1775 and the expiry of Watt's patent in 1800.

Anticipating the eventual saturation of the pumping engine market, in 1782 Watt modified his engine, patenting the sun and planet gear that enabled it to convert the up and down movement of the beam into the rotational movement needed to drive factory and mill machinery. (Watt patented the idea, but it was actually invented by William Murdock.) A previous patent by James Pickard, based on the workings of a potter's wheel (an idea some say Pickard stole from Watt in the first place) offered an alternative means of doing so, until his patent expired in 1794 and Watt could reclaim the idea. This greatly expanded the potential of the Watt machine. It meant that factories were no longer dependent upon wind, water or animal power to drive their machinery, and manufactories could locate wherever other business needs dictated.

By 1800, 308 of the 496 Boulton & Watt machines built up until that time were rotative. Some 114 of these were being used in the textile industry, along with others in ironworks, breweries and grain mills. Further improvements included the double-acting piston, whereby steam pressed on either side of the piston in turn, the improved use of expansive steam to reduce fuel consumption, and a centrifugal governor, which enabled an engine to run at a constant speed, regardless of the load being placed upon it. Savings in fuel consumption were especially important, as they made it viable to open up new mining areas away from established coalfields.

Boulton introduced one further improvement to their steam boilers, which was to have important ramifications later in the locomotive age. In about 1780 he wrote to Watt with the idea of improving the steaming efficiency of his boilers by fitting tubes to the back of the firebox, to increase the area of hot gas coming into contact with the water. He later fitted four 20in-diameter copper tubes to one of his stationary boilers. This idea had to be reinvented for locomotives, and a multi-tube boiler would become one of the reasons for *Rocket*'s success at the Rainhill Trials. One further improvement was introduced by John Wilkinson's foundry at Wrexham. His improved cylinder-boring technology enabled a closer fit between cylinder and piston, and thus gave greater power.

At last human ingenuity had found a way of harnessing steam to do useful work, but the massive and slow-working Newcomen machines were never going to lend themselves to locomotion. A whole new approach would be needed.

2

Steam Locomotion

From the earliest times, people were trying to use steam power to generate movement of one kind or another. But for many centuries nobody was able to come up with practical applications for steam-driven machinery, or the technology to make steam power viable. But by the seventeenth and eighteenth centuries it seemed as if steam-powered transport might be an idea whose time had finally come.

In the 1690s Denis Papin floated the idea of using steam to drive a piston in a bore, and suggested that this could be an alternative basis to animals for powering a carriage. (An earlier version of his idea had involved the startling use of gunpowder as a fuel!) But his failure to attract sponsorship contributed to his death in poverty and obscurity, and his idea never got built. Doctor Erasmus Darwin floated the idea of a steam carriage with both principals of the Boulton Watt Partnership, and William Symington (better known as the pioneer steamboat designer of the *Charlotte Dundas*) was causing a good deal of interest with his model steam carriage, which was being shown in Edinburgh by 1786. In 1787 Oliver Evans of Maryland, USA patented a steam engine for use in a cart or carriage (though he never built it), and there was the work of William Murdoch (of which more, shortly).

But the person now widely credited as the inventor of the steam-powered motor vehicle was a French military man, who developed a *machine a feu pour le transport de wagons et surtout de l'artillerie* or, in short, a *fardier a vapeur* (or, in English, a steam-powered version of a massively built cart, used for carrying heavy military loads including cannon barrels). *Fardier* means bearer of burdens.

Nicholas-Joseph Cugnot (1725–1804) was a French-born military inventor and engineer who served with the Austrian army during the Seven Years' War. He started researching into steam-powered army vehicles in 1765 and in 1769 built a small prototype version of his cart. This was followed the next year by a full-sized version, weighing in at some 2½ tonnes. Its design was not influenced by the work of Newcomen or Watt, rather drawing on the theoretical work of Papin.

Despite being backed by the resources of the French government (it was built at the Paris Arsenal) the vehicle was seriously flawed, for developing a powered motor vehicle involved much more than just designing a suitable engine. Other factors came into play, including suspension, braking, steering, road surfaces, tyres, vibration-free bodywork, carrying capacity and range.

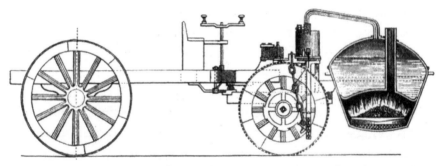

A vintage cutaway engraving of Cugnot's steam carriage (image thought to originate from an industrial encyclopedia of 1875).

Cugnot's vehicle fell short in several respects. First, it was painfully slow. It never achieved even the modest top speed claimed for it, of 4.8mph (7.8km/h), managing in trials (according to one account) just 2.25mph – less than walking pace. This was compounded by the fact that it carried no reserves of fuel or water, and had to stop every quarter of an hour or so to relight the fire, refill the boiler and raise steam afresh. There was no way of topping up the water while it was running. Nor was it helped by a boiler that was very inefficient, even by the standards of the day, leaving it with problems with maintaining pressure.

Second, it was wildly unstable. The boiler was hung in front of the single front wheel, which also carried the weight of the transmission and steering mechanisms. Some critics have calculated that, with a full boiler, the machine would simply have tipped over on its nose. Some even claimed that it actually did so, though modern replicas of the machine appear capable of movement (at least to the limited degree that the original ever was). What was certain was that the machine would have been virtually useless on the ravaged landscape of the battlefield for which it was designed.

Related to this second flaw, the machine was virtually unsteerable, since the driver had to turn the huge weight that was hung on the front wheel to direct it. During trials in 1771 it was said to have partly demolished a brick wall, with Cugnot becoming the first person ever to be prosecuted for dangerous driving (or so some accounts claim – this story did not appear until 1801).

After some inconclusive army trials and the small matter of the French Revolution, funding was withdrawn for its development and Cugnot was forced into an impoverished exile in Brussels. But, for all its shortcomings, the *fardier* was probably the first vehicle to prove that steam locomotion was a realistic possibility. Moreover, Cugnot made some specific advances in steam technology, improving engine efficiency by moving pistons without condensing steam. (His engine consisted of two 13in (33cm) 1.75 cu ft (50l) pistons. He was also the first person to successfully translate the reciprocating action, characteristic of most early steam engines, into the rotary motion needed to drive a vehicle's wheels, using a ratchet device. The full-sized version of the vehicle survives and can today be seen in the Musée des Arts et Métiers in Paris.

William Murdoch (1754–1839) (he anglicised his name to Murdock after he settled in England) was the Scottish-born son of a millwright, whose ambition from an early age was to work with steam engines. In 1777 he set out to seek employment with Boulton & Watt, walking the 300 miles to Birmingham for an interview. It seems he impressed his prospective employers, not just with his pedestrian abilities but also with a wooden hat that he had turned on a lathe of his own design. Whatever the reason, he was immediately employed by them, and remained in their employ for the rest of his life.

Boulton & Watt were based in Birmingham but had a good deal of business with the Cornish mining industries. From 1779 Murdoch was based in Redruth, Cornwall, and spent his time installing and repairing Boulton & Watt engines. He would also help Boulton & Watt enforce against anyone infringing the company's patents.

But Murdoch was not just a skilled engineer, he was a considerable inventor in his own right. Among his ideas was a steam-powered carriage. Watt, his employer, was fundamentally opposed to the use of high-pressure steam on safety grounds, but was also fearful of losing Murdoch's valuable services to his company in pursuit of this 'madcap' idea. By 1782 Boulton described him as 'the most active man and best engine erector I ever saw'. A letter from Boulton to Watt makes it clear that leaving was on Murdoch's mind. He urged Watt to dissuade Murdoch from the idea, and also to include a scheme for a steam-powered carriage in a forthcoming patent application, as a means of blocking Murdoch's plans. This Watt did, but he was highly cynical about his scheme:

> I have given such descriptions of engines for wheeled carriages as I could do in the time and space I could allow myself; but it is very defective and can only serve to keep other people from similar patents.

These 'other people' particularly included William Murdoch. For a while, pressures of the day job and domestic duties prevented Murdoch pursuing his steam-carriage ideas. But it appears that news of William Symington's carriage reached him and rekindled his enthusiasm. He set off for London to lodge his own patent, but Watt intercepted him at Exeter and per-suaded him to return home. (One thing that is not entirely clear from this is that, under their usual terms of employment, anything a Boulton & Watt employee invented would become the intellectual property of their employer. What was Murdoch going to patent and for whose benefit?)

Had Murdoch been allowed to continue with his work, the world might have had steam-powered transport twenty years sooner, but on the way back home, Murdoch did at least give a demonstration of his model carriage in the Rivers' Great Room at the King's Head Hotel, Truro – the first-ever public demonstration in Britain of steam locomotion. It is thought that Murdoch continued to work – low-key – on his project without his employer's backing, and there are some who think he even made a full-sized model.

So what was Murdoch's model carriage like? *Grace's Guide* describes it as:

> A three-wheeled vehicle about a foot in height with the engine and boiler placed between the two larger back wheels with a spirit lamp underneath to heat the water and a tiller at the front turning the smaller front wheel. The mechanics of the locomotive incorporated a number of innovations such as a boiler safety valve, having the cylinder partly immersed in the boiler and using a new valve system on the lines of the D-slide valve.

One popular story tells that Murdoch gave one of his models an outdoor trial run. It soon outpaced him and, in the course of his pursuit, Murdoch came across a highly agitated Vicar of Redruth, who had been pursued by a mysterious monster breathing fire and smoke, whom he was convinced was the devil!

In 1797 and 1798 new neighbours came to live next door to Murdoch in Redruth. They showed considerable interest in Murdoch's experiments, and had apparently even been to see the steam carriage in action prior to moving in. They were a future railway pioneer, **Andrew Vivian** and his cousin, one **Richard Trevithick.** Vivian was a mechanical engineer and mine captain who financed the first steam carriage and in 1802 was granted a joint patent for high-pressure steam locomotives. As for Trevithick …

Richard Trevithick (1771–1833) was the son of a Cornish mining captain. He showed little promise at school, being described by one of his schoolmasters as 'a disobedient, slow, obstinate, spoiled boy, frequently absent and very inattentive'. The one exception was mathematics, for which he showed an aptitude, albeit with an unconventional approach to the subject. He left school and went to work at the East Stray Park Mine. By the age of 19 he was employed as a consultant.

As we saw, as a young man he saw Murdoch's model steam carriage in action, and was influenced by it to build a full-sized version of his own. The expiry of Watt's patent in 1800 removed a major obstacle to its development. Trevithick was quick to take advantage of the freedom from patents. Indeed, even before they expired, one of his jobs was to modify his mine-

Richard Trevithick, honoured today in his native Camborne, Cornwall, former centre of the county's tin and copper mining industry.

owning employer's stationary steam engines, so as to evade Watt's royalty payments, payable under Watt's other patents. Indeed, the end of Watt's patent coincided with an upsurge in locomotive building by Trevithick and others. In fact, Trevithick spent much of his working life at odds with Boulton & Watt, partly because he tended to be a spokesman for Cornish mining interests in opposition to them, and partly for his championing of the use of 'strong' (that is, high-pressure) steam. Watt was a firm supporter of the low-pressure (or atmospheric or condensing) engine, relying on atmospheric pressure for its operation.

'High pressure' is a relative term, and what Trevithick initially meant by it was between 35 and 50psi, a very modest level of pressure compared to the locomotives that were soon to follow. But even at this level it gave four times the power of a similar-sized atmospheric engine. It also offered the possibility of building much more compact steam engines – possibly even compact enough to power a locomotive engine, as Murdoch had already demonstrated. Watt remained strongly opposed to the use of high-pressure steam and at one stage called for Trevithick to be hanged for his irresponsibility in using it.

Trevithick's first foray into 'strong steam' took the form of a stationary engine, installed near Camborne in 1800. Despite Watt's doom-laden predictions, this machine had a successful working life of seventy years. Then, on Christmas Eve 1801, Trevithick unveiled the world's first full-size road-going, steam locomotive, christened the *Puffing Devil*. He took several friends for a spin in it, up Camborne Hill, Cornwall, with Andrew Vivian at the controls. All went well until they stopped for lunch at a hostelry. They parked in a nearby barn but failed to extinguish the locomotive's fire. The resultant inferno destroyed both barn and locomotive.

Undeterred, further steam locomotives followed. The poor surface of the roads (particularly in Cornwall), and the danger of his noisy machines frightening the horses using the public highway, began to persuade Trevithick that a railway might be a more satisfactory testing ground for them.

In 1802 the Coalbrookdale Company was said to have assembled a rail locomotive to Trevithick's design. Coalbrookdale would have been an ideal place for this locomotive experiment, being a forward-looking organisation, and one of the first (if not *the* first) to go over to using the iron rails that might have taken its weight. But little is known about how it worked or what it looked like, since the only written reference to it was in a letter from Trevithick. There are no detailed engineering drawings to go on. A drawing of a (possibly) similar locomotive in the Science Museum suggests it might have had a 4½in (11.4cm) diameter cylinder, a 3ft (91.4cm) stroke and ran on a 3ft- (91.4cm-) gauge tramway.

Such sketchy details as exist of Trevithick's work at this time are also the basis for the recreation (or rather conjectural reconstruction) of the later (1804) Penydarren locomotive, now in the National Waterfront Museum in Swansea, for which no contemporary plans survive at all. What is known is that the earlier Trevithick locomotive would have been dangerous to use, with the piston rod, guide bars and other moving parts located right above the furnace door (and hence dangerously close to the fireman's head). There was apparently some sort of accident shortly after it came into use; an enquiry was held but its findings were hushed up, and the locomotive was subsequently withdrawn from railway use and converted into a stationary steam boiler. Today at least a further replica can be seen at the Blist Hills Victorian town, within the Ironbridge Gorge Museums in Shropshire.

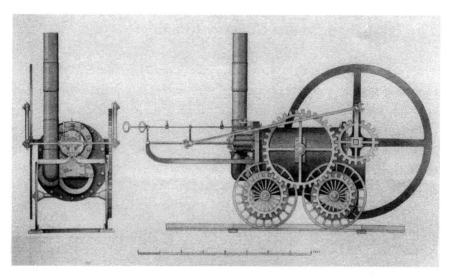

Thought to be Richard Trevithick's 1804 Penydarren locomotive – from an early engraving.

In 1803 Trevithick produced a further road-going machine, 'an improved steam engine to give motion to wheeled carriages of every description'. Arrangements were made for it to give a demonstration run in the centre of London. Oxford Street was cleared of horses and carriages for the purpose. It worked, and attracted a good deal of interest, but did not result in any orders. The ride, on its 8ft (2.5m) driving wheels without any rear suspension, was rough and the reaction of one Katherine Plymley of Shropshire was perhaps typical of public opinion:

> A man by the name of Trevithic (*sic*) has lately invented a machine to go without horses – it moves by steam; and goes with extreme velocity – the danger seems to be of the water being exhausted and of course the machine taking fire … it is I am told a very ugly and large vehicle and would be very frightful to a horse.

Henceforth, Trevithick concentrated his steam carriage efforts on railed traffic. All other considerations aside, railways could offer the prospect of a less bumpy ride than the roads of the day could provide and would encounter fewer horses to startle. It set the scene for an historic first.

The First Ever Steam Railway Journey?

The proprietor of the Penydarren ironworks near Merthyr Tydfil, Samuel Homfray, was an early steam enthusiast – he bought a share in the patents for Trevithick's locomotives in 1803. He also laid a sizeable bet (500 guineas, or £525) with fellow ironmaster Richard Crawshay that a steam locomotive could haul 10 tons of iron from the ironworks to the Glamorganshire Canal at Abercynon, a journey of 9.75 miles along the Penydarren tramroad. The background to this historic event needs a little explanation.

South Wales was something of a boom area for iron and coal production at this time and Homfray was one of several ironmasters who had lobbied for the Glamorganshire Canal to be built. Prior to its opening in 1794 the south Wales iron industry had to rely on the horse and cart to get its wares to the docks at Swansea. The canal was successful but slow, with forty-nine

PENYDARRAN IRON WORKS.

Penydarren ironworks – important scene of the first railway journey by a working locomotive (from J.G.Wood, *The Principal Rivers of Wales Illustrated*, 1813)

locks in 24 miles of canal, and it soon became severely congested, especially the length between Merthyr and the wharf at Abercynon.

But there was a clause in the Act of Parliament authorising the canal, allowing proprietors within 4 miles of the main canal to make 'collateral cuts or railways'. What the Act presumably meant was a short link of canal or railway from their factory directly to the nearest point on the canal for transhipment, but that was not what the Act said. And what the ironworks proprietors did was certainly stretching what the Act said to its extreme limits. They built 9.75 miles of tramway, completely bypassing the most congested part of the canal (coincidentally, 9.75 miles was slightly longer than the more famous length of line later completed between the two towns of Stockton and Darlington, not including the collieries section). The tramway was completed in 1802 by George Overton, the same man who later did the initial survey for the Stockton and Darlington Railway.

Trevithick had built a high-pressure stationary boiler for the Penydarren ironworks to drive a steam hammer. This boiler had wheels and driving gear added to it to turn it into a locomotive and on 21 February 1804 what is thought to be the world's first working steam train set out on its historic journey. Trevithick walked in front of it (its average speed was just 2.4mph (3.9km/h)). Trevithick describes the journey:

> Yesterday we proceeded on our journey with the engine, and we carried
> ten tons of iron in five wagons, and seventy men riding on them the whole
> of the journey ... the engine, while working, went nearly five miles an
> hour, there was no water put into the boiler from the time we started until
> our journey's end ... the coal consumed was two hundredweight.

Four hours and five minutes later the journey was complete, the bet
won and lost and history made. The journey was not without inci-
dent. Apart from breaking rails (see below) the locomotive had a bigger
loading gauge than the horse-drawn wagons that normally used the
wagonway, and various boulders and small trees had to be removed to
allow it free passage. Not least of the mysteries is how the locomotive,
with its 11ft chimney, coped with the 8ft clearance of a tunnel at the
Plymouth Ironworks, part way along the route. Radical surgery may
have been involved.

The locomotive had just about the shortest service record of any record
breaker. At 5 tons (including water) and without any suspension it proved
to be too heavy for the L-shaped tracks of the Penydarren tramroad, and
broke too many rails. On the return journey a bolt sheared, causing the
boiler to leak. The locomotive did not get back to Penydarren until the
next day (according to some accounts, allowing Crawshay to renege on
the bet, claiming that the return journey had not been completed as per
the wager).

The Cambrian newspaper of 24 July 1804 reported the event, and sensed
(rather than necessarily saw very clearly) the future:

> There can be no doubt that the number of horses in our land will be con-
> siderably reduced, and that the machine has a potential use far exceeding
> anything imagined so far for this engine.

Soon after its inaugural runs the locomotive was taken out of service and
returned to stationary duties with its steam hammer. The tramroad once
again became a purely horse-powered line (or not even that until the
broken rails had been repaired).

Unlike the designs for the Coalbrookdale locomotive, this one is
thought to have had its working parts at the opposite end to the furnace

door, making it safer to fire the locomotive whilst on the move. It had a U-shaped flue to give a larger surface area to heat up the water more efficiently. This meant the firebox and the chimney were at the same end of the locomotive and the flue ran from the firebox, through the boiler, before doubling back on itself to join the chimney.

Trevithick also had an arrangement whereby the waste steam was discharged up the chimney, functioning in effect as a blastpipe. With this, the used steam created a partial vacuum that drew heat and smoke from the firebox through the boiler, giving improved steaming. It is thought to be the first locomotive to do so and was an important feature of nearly all the steam locomotives that followed. The idea was not entirely unheard of; metal workers for centuries had been employing a similar principle, using bellows to increase the heat of their fires. What is surprising was that Trevithick failed to patent its application to locomotives. The exhaust steam also had another job to do. It was passed through the jacket in which the water being fed to the boiler was delivered, making sure the water was heated before entering the boiler.

Trevithick – Penydarren Locomotive
Built by Richard Trethivick (1803–04)
Weight: 5 tons including water
Wheels: 0-4-0 not flanged
Gauge: 4ft 2in (127cm) inside plate flanges
Cylinders: one, assumed to be horizontal. 8¼in by 4ft 6in (21cm by 137cm)
Maximum speed: 5mph
Working life: As a mobile engine, very short (days or weeks)

Trevithick went on to design other locomotives. One, for Christopher Blackell, the owner of Wylam Colliery near Newcastle, was delivered in 1805. It was built by Trevithick's agents, the Whinfield's Foundry at Gateshead. At 4½ tons, it was lighter than the Penydarren locomotive to try and overcome the track breakages problem. But this was not helped by the fact that Wylam's wagonway had wooden-edged rails, until they were replaced with iron in 1808. The locomotive was tested by the customer but not accepted, and was later converted into a blower for the foundry.

This line was to have been part of an ambitious and groundbreaking plateway, running from Newcastle to Carlisle, via Wylam (discussed in more detail in the chapter on early railways). Drawings exist of a second, modified locomotive also intended for use at Wylam, though whether it got beyond the drawing stage seems less certain.

Trevithick – Wylam Engine
Built by Whinfield's Foundry, Gateshead (1805)
Weight: 4½ tons
Cylinder: 7in by 36in (18cm by 91.5cm)
Gauge: 5ft

Another Trevithick locomotive is next on our list, this one dating from 1808. In an effort to promote public interest in steam locomotion, it ran on a purpose-built circular track just south of the modern-day Euston Square Underground station, much in the style of a fairground attraction. It certainly attracted the attention of *The Times*, who reported on it thus on 8 July 1808:

> We are credibly informed that there is a steam engine now preparing to run against any mare, horse or gelding that may be produced at the next October meeting at Newmarket. The wagers at present are stated to be 10,000:1 the engine is the favourite. The extraordinary effect of mechanical powers is already known to the world; but the novelty, singularity and powerful application against time and speed has created admiration in the minds of every scientific man. TREVITHIC [*sic*], the proprietor and patentee of the engine, has been applied to by several distinguished personages to exhibit this machine to the public, prior to it being sent to Newmarket; we have not heard this gentleman's determination yet; its greatest speed will be twenty miles in one hour and its slowest rate will never be less than 15 miles.

Part of what we know about the design of Trevithick's 1808 locomotive, christened *Catch Me Who Can*, comes from some cards he had printed, showing a side-on view of it. The purpose of these cards is not entirely clear. They do not appear to have been business cards, since they have no

A replica of Trevithick's 1808 locomotive *Catch Me Who Can*, seen at Bridgnorth on the Severn Valley Railway.

contact details. Were they tickets for admission to his London demonstration track, or for some other publicity reason, now lost in the mists of time? More generally, contemporary drawings of locomotives can sometimes be unreliable guides to their operation. Some give a faithful account of their structure from which an engineer could work. But others show fanciful working parts that would not work in practice; key details may be omitted entirely, or one part may be shown wildly out of scale with another.

Catch Me Who Can was a new locomotive, smaller than some of Trevithick's previous efforts, and pulled a four-wheeled carriage at speeds of up to 12mph. The experiment only lasted from July to September and its start was delayed by soft ground being unable to bear the weight of the locomotive and carriage. The final resting place of the locomotive is uncertain, though one theory has it that it was rescued from a scrapheap in the goods yard of Hereford station in 1882 and is now in the possession of the Science Museum. It was said to be a boiler from a stationary engine, built by the firm of Hazeldine and Rastrick, but it appears in other respects to be a double for *Catch Me Who Can*. It is even suggested that it could actually be the remains of *Catch Me Who Can*, making it the world's oldest surviving steam locomotive.

A replica currently resides at Bridgnorth, on the Severn Valley Railway. The engineer John Isaac Hawkins later gave this retrospective account of the working of the locomotive in a letter to the *Mechanics Magazine* in 1847:

> He placed a locomotive engine, weighing about ten tons, on that railway, on which I rode, with my watch in hand, at a rate of 12 miles an hour; that Mr Trevithick then gave his opinion that it would go 20 miles an hour, or more, on a straight railway; that the engine was exhibited at one shilling admittance, including a ride for the few who were not too timid; that it ran for some weeks, when a rail broke and occasioned the engine to fly off in a tangent and overturn, the ground being very soft at the time.
>
> Mr Trevithick, having expended all his means in erecting the works and inclosure, and the shillings not having come in fast enough to pay current expenses, the engine was not set again on the rail.

Trevithick took on a variety of other projects, including a tunnel under the Thames (it was never completed, and a similar project nearly claimed the life of Isambard Kingdom Brunel). Steam ships and a variety of industrial processes made use of his high-pressure steam engines. In 1816 he left for South America, where one of his engines had proved to be successful in clearing water from a Peruvian silver mine (Watt's atmospheric engines being virtually useless at high altitude). After an eventful, and by no means successful, time there he returned to England in 1827, penniless. Robert Stephenson, who came across him whilst in South America, had to fund him the £50 he needed for his return fare home.

Back in England, he sought a pension from the government – something given to many other distinguished inventors – but it was refused him. His last project was a steamship being built in Dartford, Kent. This was the one that was to have incorporated a giant version of a reaction turbine – essentially an aeolipile (Hero of Alexandria's invention of almost 2,000 years before). Trevithick died in 1833 of pneumonia and only narrowly avoided being buried in a pauper's grave in Dartford. His workmates organised a collection to pay for his funeral.

John Blenkinsop and the Middleton Colliery Rack Locomotives 1812–14

The railway at Middleton Colliery was initially horse-drawn, but the Napoleonic wars led to sharp increases in the price of horses and fodder, forcing those who relied on horses for haulage to consider radical alternatives. One such was **John Blenkinsop**, the then manager of the Middleton Colliery. In 1812 he placed an order for a steam locomotive with a Leeds company, Fenton Murray and Wood (then one of the country's leading builders of steam engines, rivalling Boulton & Watt).

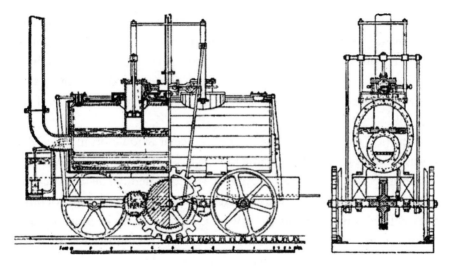

Salamanca – a cutaway diagram of the rack and pinion locomotive supplied to the Middleton Railway in 1812. It was destroyed by a boiler explosion in 1818. The illustration is thought to have come from a French technical magazine, *Bulletin de la Societe d'encouragement pour l'industrie Nationale*, dating from 1815.

One of the issues for them was whether smooth iron wheels would provide sufficient adhesion to pull loads along smooth iron tracks, particularly up steep inclines like those around the Middleton Collieries. The Penydarren experiment was by no means conclusive on that score. Another consideration was that, in order to minimise rail breakages, the locomotive would have to be lighter, and therefore have less adhesion. More to the point, Blenkinsop had taken out the patent for a rack-and-pinion railway system in 1811. It would be the first railway of its kind, but the principle was simple. A third, toothed rail was attached to the outside of the track and engaged with a cogwheel on the locomotive to pull the locomotive along. Blenkinsop did not specify any particular means of propulsion for his system, beyond saying that, 'A steam engine is greatly to be preferred.' Quite what alternative (if any) he had in mind is not clear.

Blenkinsop railed against making royalty payments as a result of Trevithick's patent on high-pressure steam, claiming that 'he considered his patent in no way connected with their [patent] grant'. Whether Blenkinsop did more than just complain about it is not clear.

If the colliery owners could be persuaded to use the rack system, Blenkinsop stood to benefit from his own patent royalties. It would be no small matter for them to foot the bill for the special rails and locomotives it needed, but the gradients involved in this particular case would probably have defeated any conventional locomotive of the day. So the system was adopted and proved to be a success, capable of moving 90-ton loads at 4mph.

Their first locomotive made its appearance at Middleton in June 1812. It was thought to have been named *Prince Regent* (or *Blenkinsop*). A second locomotive was introduced in August 1812, named *Salamanca* after one of the Duke of Wellington's victories of that year. Two other locomotives, delivered in 1813 and 1814, were thought to have been named *Lord Wellington* and *Marquis Wellington*. But there is some confusion about this as they may just have been nicknames given them by the workforce. In any event the Middleton colliery became the first commercial organisation in the world to operate steam engines successfully.

This was the time of the Luddites, and the replacement of men and horses with machines was not universally welcomed. Attempts were made to sabotage the new line and some damage was done. But, despite a reward of 50 guineas (£52.50) being offered, a year's wages for a working man, to catch the guilty parties, nobody was ever charged for the offence.

Blenkinsop: *Prince Regent* Locomotive
Built by Fenton, Murray and Wood of Leeds (1812)
Wheels: 4 (non-driving) 3ft 6in (100.7cm) diameter
Cylinders: 8in by 20in (20.3cm by 50.8cm)
Boiler pressure: 55psi
Weight: 5 tons (estimated)
Maximum speed: 10mph with a 20-ton load
(These vital statistics come from Stretton – others differ in detail.)

Apart from the rack system, which was Blenkinsop's own patent, the design of the locomotives seems to have been all Matthew Murray's own work. Dendy Marshall describes it as 'quite original' and says that its general arrangement was followed by every locomotive for the next sixteen years. They also appear to have been durable; a Murray-type locomotive (albeit without the rack but otherwise an exact replica of the 1822 original, built in 1851–52) was reported as being in use as late as 1912. This was, however, probably *Lyon*, whose operational dates are remarkably similar to these. More immediately, George Stephenson's first locomotive, *My Lord*, was considerably influenced by the Blenkinsop and Murray designs of 1812.

Turning to other mechanical features of the Middleton locomotives, the drive arrangements on them sound anything but direct. They had two vertical cylinders set into the boiler fore and aft along the centreline. These drove crosshead beams with connecting rods going down each side of the boiler to cranks on cross-shafts, which drove gears between the frames below the centreline of the boiler. These in turn drove another cross-shaft connected to the drive cog on the left-hand side outside the frame. One feature on the Middleton locomotives that was to become standard on all subsequent locomotives was to have at least two cylinders, set at 90 degrees to each other so that wherever in its cycle the engine stopped, one of the cylinders would always be on a power stroke and the locomotive could pull away. Trevithick's Penydarren locomotive had only a single cylinder and consequently had to have an expensive and heavy flywheel to carry the engine over the flat spots in its cycle.

In 1812 William Chapman and his brother Edward were granted a patent for an idea so similar to Blenkinsop's rack rail that Blenkinsop called it 'mechanical larceny'. This involved laying a length of chain between the rails for the entire length or the railway. A specially adapted locomotive would engage with the chain and winch itself along the chain, much as a rack locomotive would engage with the rack. However, initial tests with the new system were not encouraging. The locomotive involved eventually evolved into the *Steam Elephant*.

But, to return to the rack railway proper, the local press were enthusiastic about the Middleton Railway's maiden run:

> At four o'clock in the afternoon the machine ran from the Coal-staith to the top of Hunslet Moor, where six, and afterwards eight, wagons of coal, each weighing 3 ¼ tons, were hooked onto the back part. With this immense weight, to which, as it approached the town, was super-added about fifty of the spectators, mounted upon the wagon, it started on its return to the Coal-staith and performed the journey, a distance of about a mile and a half, principally on a dead level, in 25 minutes, without the slightest accident. The experiment, which was witnessed by thousands of spectators, was crowned with complete success; and when it is considered that the invention is applicable to all rail-roads, and that upon the works of Mr Brandling alone the use of fifty horses will be dispensed with, and the corn necessary for the consumption of at least 200 men saved, we cannot forbear to hail the invention as one of vast public utility, and to rank the inventor amongst the benefactors of his country.
>
> *Leeds Mercury*, 27 June 1812

On the safety front, the Middleton locomotives were fitted with not one but two safety valves, spring-loaded and adjustable by means of a nut. It was, as Dendy Marshall says:

> An arrangement much more suitable for a locomotive than valves held down by a weight on the end of a lever, used by Stephenson several years later (e.g. the Rocket, 1829)

But even this did not make them totally safe – or tamper-proof. Being the world's first railway meant they were able to secure more firsts (not all of them welcome ones). Driving a locomotive could be particularly risky. On 28 February 1818 the locomotive *Salamanca* blew up as a result of folly by the driver, who had fastened the safety valves down for extra power. The *Leeds Mercury* reported the matter, with an eye for gruesome detail, thus:

> Fatal accident – on Wednesday afternoon one of the locomotive engines of the Middleton Colliery, was burst by the pressure of the steam. The shock produced by the explosion was so great that it was felt by every house in Hunslet, and the unfortunate engine driver was literally blown to atoms, and his mutilated body scattered in all directions.
>
> *Leeds Mercury*, 15 February 1834

They added for good measure that the driver was 'carried, with great violence, into an adjoining field the distance of one hundred yards'. The Middleton employed the world's first regular railway engine driver, a former surface pit labourer named James Hewitt, who had been trained by the locomotive company's test driver. He later (12 February 1834) became an early railway staff fatality, after the poorly maintained boiler on his locomotive exploded.

Stories of engine drivers blowing themselves up by tampering with the locomotive's safety valves to squeeze more performance out of them are a depressingly familiar part of early railway history. The first safety valve was developed not for a locomotive but for a pressure cooker, by Denis Papin in 1679. The early locomotive safety valves were seen as one of the driver's optional controls, allowing him to adjust them according to the load being placed on the engine. On many early models, the driver simply had to slide a weight along a lever, to increase (or decrease) the pressure under which the boiler operated. Trevithick suffered an early explosion in Greenwich in 1803, when the boy trained to tend a stationary engine abandoned his post to go fishing for eels. Since 1806 Trevithick had been fitting his boilers with two safety valves, one of them inaccessible to the driver but set to be a failsafe, being activated at a slightly higher pressure than the other accessible one.

Lever and other weighted-type safety valves tended to be over-sensitive to the rough riding of early locomotives. They would bounce and let off steam at any imperfection in the track (of which there was no shortage). They were soon phased out on locomotives, and one solution was to use a spring, rather than a weight, to control them. Timothy Hackworth was the first to use this on his *Royal George* of 1828. They could still be tampered with, and one solution to this was to make them inaccessible by enclosing them in a brass case, which also stopped the hot steam blowing all over the crew. But the idea of the safety valve being a legitimate and adjustable part of the driver's controls still persisted in some quarters until well into the 1850s. Not until 1855 would a safety valve that was both reliable and tamper-resistant be introduced, by John Ramsbottom, the Locomotive Superintendent of the London and North Western Railway. But even these would not be totally immune to fatal explosions.

Whilst on the subject of fatalities, there is another unwelcome first for the Middleton Railway. The first member of the public claimed to have been killed by a locomotive was a 13-year-old boy, John Bruce, knocked down in February 1813 whilst running alongside the tracks at Middleton. The *Leeds Mercury* unsympathetically reported that it would operate 'as a warning to others'.

Blenkinsop was keen to promote the savings to be had from what he referred to as 'his' machine. This from a letter to a fellow colliery overseer, John Watson:

> I write to inform you that my Patent Steam carriage is daily at work and is capable of moving 20 coal wagons each weighing 3 ½ tons at the rate of 3 ½ miles an hour = 74 tons including the weight of the machine ...
>
> The quantity of inferior coals used in 12 hours is 10 cwt. – 45 cwt of the same coals would sell for 12/6 – therefore the coals used in all 2/9 per day.
>
> Letter, 2 August 1812

In a letter to the *Monthly Magazine* Blenkinsop also indulged in some blatant free advertising. His letter concludes:

> The use of these steam carriages has given the greatest satisfaction and they promise to be attended with the most beneficial effects, particularly as it is clearly ascertained that at least five-sixths of the expense of conveying goods by horses will be saved by the invention.
>
> *Monthly Magazine*, June 1814

George Stephenson came to visit the Middleton railway, and it attracted international interest. In August 1816 *The Times* reported a visit by a Lieutenant-Colonel Fischer of Schafhausen, a German iron manufacturer:

At Leeds he notices the wagons driven by steam, which conveyed coal along an iron railway, three miles in length, to the town. 'I went to meet this train' said he 'Two miles off, and when I came up to it the man who guided the whole desired me to mount the wagon of the machine, which was provided with seats; and the usual rate of its motion being such, that a man walking rather fast can scarcely keep up with it; in order to satisfy my curiosity he increased its rapidity to that of a trotting horse, by a stronger application of steam to put in motion the stampers which moved at the rate of 80 strokes in a minute. I was very glad when he made it move more slowly, as I was afraid of an explosion, because the steam hissed as though our vehicle was drawn along by half-a-dozen of broken-winded horses. For the rest, I rejoiced to enter Leeds seated in this triumphal car of human ingenuity (or so I would call it) where the elements confined in so small a compass themselves compel 23 waggons laden with 60 cwt of coal each.'

The rack railway was not an unqualified success. The Blenkinsop system was fairly expensive to install and operate and the rack system itself was subject to heavy wear, which impacted on its reliability. One of the things Murray, the Middleton engines' designer, disliked about the rack arrangement was having the third rail running along the outside of the track, rather than down the middle, between the rails. This was forced on him by the fact that horses might also have wanted to use the line, and a central rack would form an unacceptable tripping hazard. Whilst the side track for the rack may work for the horses, it created side pull and distortion, adding to wear and resistance on the mechanism. Nonetheless, the rack system continued to operate at Middleton until about 1835, when for some reason (possibly the second boiler explosion, referred to earlier?) the use of steam at the colliery was abandoned entirely, apart from a single stationary engine. The railway was worked by horses until 1866. The rack system has now fallen into disuse, except for specialised applications such as mountain railways.

The Stephensons and the Hetton Colliery Railway

Hetton Colliery Railway has a number of claims to fame. It was the first railway to be designed from the start to be operated totally by machines, and it was also the first completely new line to be developed by George Stephenson. He was helped in this by Robert Stephenson (his brother, not George's equally famous son). It pre-dated by three years the Stockton and Darlington line, by which George made his reputation. It was (briefly) the world's longest railway at 8 miles (12.6km), and by the time of its closure in 1959 it was the oldest mineral railway in Britain. It was also enormously influential internationally, attracting many would-be railway builders from around the world.

It was developed to carry coal extracted from the eastern half of the Durham coalfield to Sunderland, from where it could be shipped to its various markets. The area was no stranger to mineral railways. The first wagonway on the Wear was laid by Thomas Allan in 1693 and as early as 1793 a single stretch of the Wear had ten coal staiths connected by rail to some thirty pits. Work on the railway began before any coal had been dug from the coalfields it was intended to serve. They were not even certain at that stage that there were economic reserves of coal of a sufficiently high quality and accessibility to be extracted. They need not have worried – by 1826, it was delivering some 79,000 chaldrons (Newcastle cartloads) of coal per year.

George Stephenson was hired to design the railway and his brother, Robert, was made resident engineer, to oversee its construction. George decided on a shorter, more aggressively engineered route for the railway, deciding that this would be more cost-effective than the flatter, but longer, alternative. This route involved a hill, requiring a pair of stationary engines that pulled trucks up it in groups of eight, and five self-acting inclines, in which empty wagons were pulled uphill by the weight of full ones descending it.

Hetton Colliery officially opened on 18 November 1822. In the following year, disappointment grew at the fact that the line was not achieving its design capacity, leading to the dismissal of Robert Stephenson Senior. George Stephenson initially sold five of his locomotives to the colliery, but they were not particularly successful and were replaced in the 1830s. But one locomotive that may have had a longer career there was built for the company in 1822. Reference was made to it in the section on the Middleton Collieries Railway. It continued working until 1912, making it at that time the world's oldest working locomotive. Or was it? It is now claimed that the locomotive, today housed in the National Railway Museum in York, is not the 1822 original, designed by Nicholas Wood, but one of a pair of 1851–52 replicas of it, built for Nicholas' son, Sir Lindsay Wood (the other having been lost in a boiler explosion in 1858–59).

The railway carried its last coal in September 1959 and the last 90ft of track was lifted in November 1960.

Brunton's Mechanical Traveller. Also known as the Steam Horse, it must count as one of the more eccentric contributions to early railway technology. It was said to be one of the responses to the increasing cost and scarcity of horses and fodder, brought about by the Napoleonic Wars. Businesses that had hitherto seen steam locomotives as a 'noisy and dangerous novelty' were starting to regard them as a serious alternative to horses. But one problem in hilly areas was their limited hill-climbing capability. Even steam enthusiasts such as Robert Stephenson and William Hedley thought the locomotives of the day incapable of climbing anything steeper than a 1 in 100 slope. Any steeper incline would in their view require either a cumbersome fixed engine or an expensive rack-and-pinion system.

This was a problem for the Butterley Ironworks Company, which faced an incline of 1 in 50 between its limestone quarry at Crich and the Cromford Canal, some 1.25 miles away. A solution seemed to present itself in the form of a patent taken out in May 1813 by an engineer (then employed by Butterley) named William Brunton, for a locomotive that walked along the track, using two steam-driven 'legs'. Butterley ordered one and it was delivered at a cost of £240. From the few records we have, it appears to have worked satisfactorily, to the extent that Newbottle Colliery in County Durham ordered a much larger two-cylinder version. According to accounts, it showed itself capable of pulling loads up a 1 in 36 gradient at 3mph, but there were other (unspecified) problems with it.

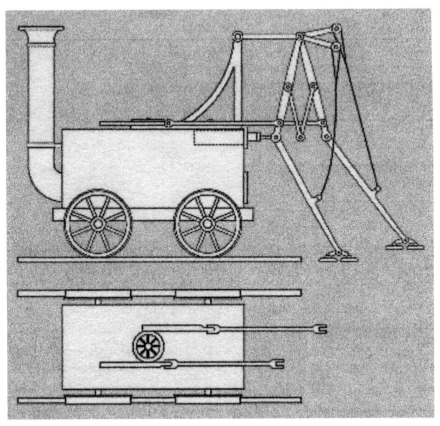

Schematic drawing of Brunton's 'walking' engine 1813.

Quite how it worked remains something of a mystery. According to Dendy Marshall, the mechanism on the drawing supplied as part of the patent application could not have made it move. Others, including *Locomotives in Profile*, professed to understand its workings, which they explained thus:

A horizontal cylinder is connected to one of the legs at the knee. When the piston is driven back, it presses the leg against the ground, and thus propels the engine forward. As the engine advances, the leg straightens and as the limit of the step is reached it causes the arm above to rise; this pulls a cord, which lifts the foot from the ground. The action of the other leg is similar but the motion is derived from the first leg, not the cylinder.

A rod attached above the knee of the first leg is connected to a toothed rack. This rotates a cogwheel on the centreline of the boiler, which operates a rack on the other side with a rod from this attached to the second leg. When the piston is driven out and pushes the first leg the left rack is drawn backward, turning the cogwheel which pulls the right rack forward and operates the second leg in the same way as the piston rod does on the first one, and thus the legs take alternate steps, and walk the engine forward.

Locomotives in Profile, 2008

I trust that is all perfectly clear.

According to the most colourful account of what happened one fateful day, an event was being organised by the River Wear at Newbottle in July 1815 to celebrate the Duke of Wellington's victory at Waterloo. The Mechanical Traveller was one of the diversions on display and the crowd were urging the operator on to ever greater efforts. He made the 'horse' 'canter' and 'gallop', according to some (almost certainly unreliable) witnesses reaching speeds of up to 30mph. In a search for more power the operator made the usual fatal error of screwing the safety valve down. Inevitably the boiler exploded, killing thirteen (some say fifteen) people and injuring forty-three others. It went down in history as the world's first railway disaster (though two boys 'slain with a wagon' on a wooden mine railway at Whickham, County Durham, in 1650 might have a prior claim to that melancholy distinction). Enthusiasm for the Steam Horse went into a fatal decline thereafter. Brunton went on to become a partner in the Eagle Foundry, where he invented the rather more successful mechanical stoker for ships.

Brunton's Mechanical Traveller (Mark 1)
Built by William Brunton (1813)
Wheels: 4, not driven (and two steam-driven legs)
Weight: 2.3 tons
Boiler pressure: 40psi
Cylinders: one at 6in by 24in (152mm by 610mm)
Maximum speed: officially 3 mph (4.8km/h)

Steam Elephant only came to light in modern times in 1931. Possibly the earliest known oil painting of a steam locomotive was later found in the possession of a local school and was acquired by the Beamish Museum in 1995. It was at the time of its discovery thought to be the work of George Stephenson, being built to his standard 4ft 8½in standard gauge for the Wallsend Waggonway. It was a six-wheeled locomotive with a centre-flue boiler and a notably long, tapered chimney, the lower part of which incorporated a feedwater heater (as seen on an early Trevithick locomotive). It is driven by two vertical cylinders, set into the top centreline.

Two replicas. *Steam Elephant* and, behind it, *Puffing Billy* at Beamish Open Air Museum. (Darrin Antrobus CC SA 2.0 via WikimediaCommons)

It is now thought to have been the work of John Buddle (the Manager of Wallsend Colliery) and William Chapman, and dated from 1815. It was not spectacularly successful at Wallsend, probably due to lack of adhesion on their wooden rails, nor during a trial period at Washington, for the same reason. But it came into its own once Wallsend got iron rails and served there at least into the mid 1820s. It then appears to have been rebuilt and served for another decade at the Hetton Collieries. A working replica was completed from paintings and other contemporary material by Beamish Open Air Museum in 2002.

Steam Elephant
Built by John Buddle and William Chapman (1815)
Weight: 7.5 tons (9 tons after rebuild)
Cylinders: one of 9in by 24in (230mm by 610mm)
Top speed: 4.5mph (7km/h)
Load capacity: 90 tons over short distances

Puffing Billy **and the Wylam locomotives** were also produced in the north-east. The village of Wylam and its colliery (about 10 miles (16km) west of Newcastle) holds an important place in the history of steam loco-motion. It was where **George Stephenson** was born, whose birthplace can still be found a mile east of the village centre (now National Trust, but not open to the public). The colliery was also the home of two other major figures in steam history. **Timothy Hackworth** was the son of the colliery's foreman blacksmith, and a colleague of George Stephenson. He worked at the Stephensons' Forth Street works in Newcastle, his loco-motive, *Sans Pareil*, was a finalist in the Rainhill trials and he became locomotive Superintendent and manager of the Stockton and Darlington Railway. **William Hedley** and colleagues designed and built *Puffing Billy*, which pre-dated Stephenson's first engine by two years and is the world's oldest surviving steam locomotive (now in the Science Museum).

Even the local railway bridge has a claim to historical fame. This 1876 structure is one of the world's first rib-arch railway bridges and is Listed Grade 2★. It has even been claimed that it introduced new deve-lopments in bridge building that paved the way for the Tyne Bridge at Newcastle (1928) and Sydney Harbour Bridge (1932). However, whilst there is a superficial resemblance between them there are significant dif-ferences in their structural details.

The lords of the manor, the Blackett family, were associated with the village from 1659 to the mid twentieth century. They had a long and entrepreneurial relationship with its colliery, building one of the north of England's earliest wagonways in 1748. This carried coal from the pithead to the staiths at Lemington, on the Tyne. More particularly, they were great champions of steam innovation.

Their involvement with steam started when news of Richard Trevithick's Penydarren locomotive reached Christopher Blackett, the then proprietor of Wylam Colliery. He ordered a locomotive from Trevithick, which was built to his design b y Whinfield's Foundry in Gateshead, owned by John Whinfield, Trevithick's agent in the north-east. John Steele, who had worked on the Penydarren locomotive, oversaw the building of this one. At 4½ tons it was lighter than the Penydarren locomotive, with the aim of avoiding broken rails. It had Wylam's gauge of 5ft (not common elsewhere in the north-east) and flanged wheels for running on edge rails.

The problem was that Wylam's edge rails were wooden, and unlikely to bear the weight of this or any other locomotive. Wylam relaid its tracks in 1808 as a 5ft-gauge plateway, partly inspired by the grand plan of a local landowner, William Thomas. He wanted to build a plateway between Newcastle and Carlisle, with the Wylam wagonway forming part of the route (see the details in the chapter on early railways). The locomotive only had demonstration runs in the maker's yard and never set wheels on Wylam tracks. It was not accepted by Blackett, and was converted into a blower for an iron foundry.

There is talk of another Trevithick locomotive designed for Wylam, and a drawing exists in the Science Museum. It was similar – but not identical – to the original Wylam locomotive, and the gauge is shown as Wylam's unique 5ft. But there seems to be no hard evidence of it ever having being built. It could have been an alternative design for the one that was built.

But Blackett's enthusiasm had not been dampened by the lack of success with Trevithick's locomotive. He approached Trevithick about building another one, but he was too busy to undertake the commitment. So Blackett decided to see what they could do in-house, and gave the job to his superintendent at Wylam, William Hedley. The question of whether a smooth-wheeled locomotive had sufficient traction to pull a train on smooth rails was not yet resolved. They briefly considered using a rack–rail system, but the cost of converting all 5 miles of their wagonway to the rack system would have been a prohibitive £8,000.

So in 1813 a hand-cranked trolley, powered by four men, was set up by Hedley for experimental purposes, which established on a scientific basis that a locomotive could move a viable load with smooth wheels on smooth rails. These lessons were then converted into a test locomotive (possibly using parts from the failed earlier example). It was delivered in spring 1813, by Thomas Waters of Gateshead. It was not a complete success, and it is thought that it may have been this locomotive that George Stephenson saw, and which persuaded him that he could do better himself. It may also be a basis for Hedley to claim that he was the father of the practical steam locomotive, since he pre-dated Stephenson's locomotive, *Blucher*. The rack locomotives were a technological blind alley and Trevithick's earlier Penydarren locomotive was a once-only trip.

An important image of *Puffing Billy*, the world's oldest surviving steam locomotive, pictured some time before 1862 (when it was retired to the Science Museum).

These experiments led to William Hedley designing a second locomotive, which was built by Jonathan Foster, Wylam Colliery's engine-wright. This was the famous *Puffing Billy*, unveiled in March 1814. Unlike its predecessors, it had vertical cylinders at the back and outside the boiler, kept warm by steam jackets. The drive from them was transmitted via 'grasshopper' beams running fore and aft and driving a single crankshaft, from which gears drove and coupled the wheels to improve traction. The boiler was wrought iron with a return flue to improve steaming (which had been a problem with the earlier experimental Wylam locomotive). It had a tender attached to the front (chimney and firebox) end, which carried the water and coal, not to mention the fireman. The driver had his footplate at the opposite end of the locomotive. *Puffing Billy* gets its name from the distinctive noise made by the locomotive's blastpipes (and, it is suggested, it was named after asthmatic William 'Billy' Hedley). The noise from it was apparently so loud that local farmers complained of it disturbing livestock in the nearby fields, and the colliery was forced to find ways of quietening it down.

Puffing Billy, 1813.

Puffing Billy started life as a four-wheeler, but its weight proved excessive for the plateway tracks of the day, and it was rebuilt in 1815 with eight coupled wheels carried on two power bogies to spread the load. It was returned to its original four-wheeled format in about 1830, when the colliery tracks were replaced with stronger edge rails.

Apart from its early tendency to break rails, *Puffing Billy* was also slow, being capable of no more than 5mph (8km/h). Despite this, it continued in service until 1862 when Edward Blackett lent it to the Patent Office Museum in London (now the Science Museum). He later sold it to them (for £20, after arguing that it could still do useful work). George

Puffing Billy at the Science Museum, London. The most famous (and the oldest surviving) pre-Stephenson locomotive.

Stephenson, who lived locally, was said to have been influenced by it, and its success was an important factor in the cause of steam locomotion. It can still be seen at London's Science Museum and a working replica is operated at the Beamish Open Air Museum. *Puffing Billy* was modified and rebuilt several times during its long working life and it is a moot point how much of the Science Museum exhibit is original.

Puffing Billy
Built by William Hedley, Jonathan Forster and Timothy Hackworth (1813–14)
Driving wheels diameter: 39in (99.1cm)
Gauge: 5ft
Weight: 8.38 tons
Boiler pressure: 50psi
Cylinders: 2
Cylinder size: 9in by 36in (22.9cm by 91.4cm)
Maximum speed 5mph
Retired: 1862

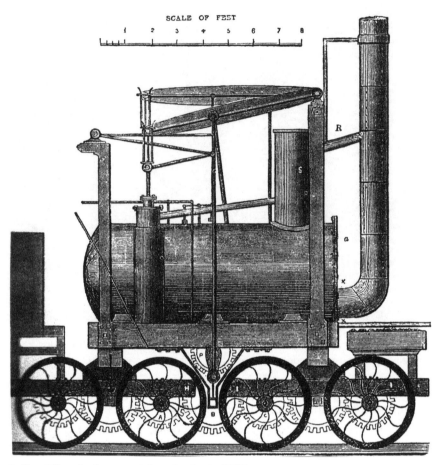

Puffing Billy, rebuilt as an eight-wheeler in 1815.

Puffing Billy was followed by two other locomotives built at Wylam –
Wylam Dilly and *Lady Mary*. They were modelled on *Billy*, but with
improvements. Like *Billy*, they underwent the transformation from four
to eight wheels and back to four flanged wheels, as the tracks changed,
and were also heavily modified during their long working lives. Timothy
Hackworth, who was foreman smith at Wylam when these locomotives
were being built, also claimed credit for them. *Dilly* (the name 'dilly'
was that given to the trucks used on the wagonway, and also to locomotives produced there) was used from 1822 as the engine of a paddle
steamer, which in turn was used to break a strike of boatmen on the
River Tyne. In this role she was required to be accompanied by armed
guards, for fear that irate strikers would push her into the river.

Wylam Dilly, one of the Wylam locomotives, now at the Museum of Scotland, Edinburgh.

This aside, she worked on the rails of the Wylam wagonway for most of her almost seventy-year working life. She was transferred to the Craghead Colliery in 1862 and presented to the Edinburgh Museum of Science and Art (now the National Museum of Scotland) in 1883, where she is still on display. *Lady Mary* did not survive. It is thought she might have been cannibalised for spare parts on a later model.

George Stephenson and *Blucher*

The period 1808 to 1815 saw a great increase in activity related to steam power. This was largely due to circumstances relating to the Napoleonic Wars – the aforementioned increased demand for (and hence cost of) horses and fodder, and labour shortages putting a premium on manpower and productivity. George Stephenson, now working at the Killingworth Colliery, was making creative use of steam, but mainly with stationary engines. In one flooded new shaft Stephenson took a Newcomen engine, already improved by Smeaton, and further improved it so that within three days the shaft was pumped dry. In another, he was one of the first to use steam engines underground for haulage, rather than pumping. By hauling coal wagons up an inclined plane by steam power, rather than by men or boys pushing them, he was able to increase the productivity of the mine. Above ground, Stephenson made further improvements unrelated to steam power, such as a self-acting inclined plane linking the pithead with the staiths at Willington Quay.

But the age of steam locomotion was not to pass him by for much longer. In September 1813 a cog rail system was opened for use at the pit where George's brother, Robert, was the colliery engine man. The opening of an early steam-hauled mineral railway could be the occasion for a major local celebration, and the inauguration of the service to Kenton and Coxlodge collieries, on 1 September 1813, was no exception, as Sykes' *Local Records of Remarkable Events* reports:

An early George Stephenson locomotive, *Blucher*, from an early nineteenth-century engraving.

An ingenious and highly interesting experiment was performed in the presence of a vast concourse of spectators, on the railway leading from the collieries of Kenton and Coxlodge, near Newcastle, by the application of a steam engine, constructed by Messrs. Fenton, Murray and Wood, of Leeds, under the direction of Mr John Blenkinsop, the patentee, for the purpose of drawing the coal wagons. About one o' clock the new invention was set agoing, having attached to it sixteen chaldron wagons loaded with coals, each wagon with its contents weighing four tons or thereabouts, making altogether an aggregate weight little short of seventy tons. Upon a perfectly level road the machine so charged, it was computed, would travel at the rate of 3 ½ miles an hour, but in the present instance the speed was short of that, owing no doubt to some partial ascents in the railroad. Under all the circumstances it was highly approved of, and its complete success anticipated. After the experiment was finished a large party of gentlemen connected with coal mining partook of an excellent dinner provided at the Grand Stand for the occasion, when the afternoon was spent in the most agreeable and convivial manner.

Among the crowd witnessing this event was almost certainly George Stephenson. But he was unlikely to have been invited to the dinner afterwards, since he was at this time a humble employee, and thus not a 'gentleman'.

That same month, Sir Thomas Liddell, the owner of Killingworth Colliery and George Stephenson's employer, instructed him to build a steam 'travelling engine' at the West Moor Colliery workshop, to run on the Killingworth wagonway ('instructed' may have been the wrong word, since Stephenson no doubt lobbied for this to happen). Stephenson looked at the existing examples and the choices they offered. He opted for the Wylam model of wheel-on-rail (rather than rack rail) traction, with flanged wheels running on edge rails. Following the example of the Blenkinsop/Murray engine, he chose two cylinders rather than one, since a single cylinder would have needed a heavy flywheel to maintain motion when the piston reached the end of its length of travel. Two-cylinder locomotives gave a smoother drive, despite using more steam and costing more to build.

Perhaps less wisely, he opted for a single large flue to heat the water in his boiler, rather than following Trevithick's model of a U-shaped double flue that heated the water much more efficiently. The consequence of this

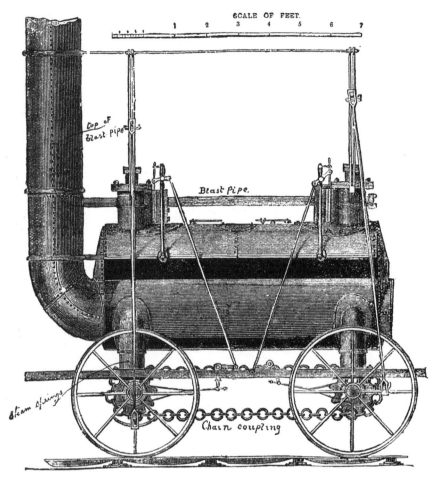

George Stephenson's 1816 Killingworth engine.

was that this locomotive, and some of the Killingworth locomotives that followed it, were chronically short of steam. One reason for this may have been a mistaken desire to avoid paying the owner of Trevithick's patent the £30 royalty he was due for the use of his modification.

Another problem with the locomotive was that the cogwheel arrangement for distributing power to the wheels was not very efficient, suffered from heavy wear and was very noisy. This inefficiency Stephenson eventually overcame by having crank pins fitted to the driving wheels, which turned by the action of hinged rods connecting the cranks to the pistons. This was not new technology – it had been used to turn flywheels on stationary engines – but this did not stop

Stephenson and Ralph Dodds (the colliery overseer) from patenting it for use on locomotives in 1815.

As an aside, a patent in those days was no small undertaking. They could only be taken out by 'gentlemen', not least because of the huge cost involved (£100 to £120 for England alone – add Scotland and Ireland and the cost rose to £350). Adding a co-inventor cost a further £24 and an extension to a patent required an Act of Parliament (with an eye-watering further payment of up to £700, and could only be pursued if you had political influence). Any patent involved no fewer than seven parts of government, each of which required payment. Even a patent search was fraught with difficulty since, until 1853, patents were not formally printed, published or even indexed.

Some of the locomotive's other shortcomings were due to the limitations of the technology of the day. The rails were not able to support the heavy early locomotives; nor could the foundries make leaf springs strong enough to support a 5-ton locomotive body, or crank axles able to stand up to extended use. They were not helped by the use of vertical cylinders on many of the early locomotives. Apart from the curiously unstable swaying ride it gave, these imposed additional wear and breakage on the tracks with their unequal downward thrusts on to the rails. Stephenson addressed the problem with the rails by a new design of chairs and a half lap joint between the rails to replace the earlier butt joints. The question of suspension for the boiler was addressed by using steam pressure from the boiler to provide a form of 'steam spring' suspension. These improvements (steam spring suspension was not entirely successful) formed a further patent application, made in September 1816 with the iron founder William Losh of Newcastle.

Despite these initial shortcomings, Stephenson's first locomotive worked quite as well as any of the other pioneers. His first effort, called *My Lord,* was completed in July 1814 and a second followed shortly afterwards, which he named *Blucher* (probably after the Prussian Field Marshal and military ally of the Duke of Wellington against Napoleon, a name also given to a former pit village, now part of Newcastle. A further possible derivation for the name was a Northumbrian dialect word for a 'huge animal'). From 1813 the smithy at West Moor became a locomotive workshop. Over the next seven years, at least sixteen locomotives were built there, including four for Killingworth itself. *Blucher* itself did not survive. Stephenson cannibalised it for spare parts as he developed more advanced models.

The year 1815 brought an end to the Napoleonic Wars and with it horse and fodder prices returning back to normal levels. This in turn brought about a cooling of enthusiasm for steam locomotion. In the following few years, Ross describes George Stephenson as 'the only person making a serious and consistent effort to develop a steam-powered railway', though even his efforts were focused on the low-speed coal-hauling variety. Without the Stephensons the Stockton and Darlington might have gone ahead with its original plan to be horse-drawn and the Liverpool and Manchester might have stuck to its original decision to use a combination of horse power and stationary steam engines. Even so, by 1825 the Stephensons had only built a total of sixteen steam locomotives (and not even all of these can be accounted for from surviving records).

In 1817 he supervised the manufacture of the first locomotive to run in Scotland – a six-wheeler built for the Duke of Portland, to run on

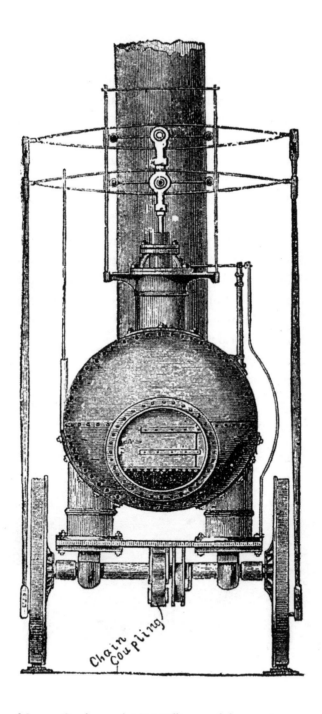

Front view of George Stephenson's 1816 Killingworth locomotive.

the Kilmarnock and Troon railway. The locomotive – named *The Duke* – failed in a number of respects. It could only pull 10 tons at 5mph; the central cog had a tendency to catch on high points on the track, bending the axles and connecting rods; and it proved, like many of its predecessors, to be too heavy for the rails, leading to breakages. In short, it proved to be no better (and in some respects worse) than the horses it replaced, and was quickly withdrawn.

As we saw, in 1820 the Hetton Coal Company announced plans to sink a new pit in County Durham, to be served by an 8-mile railway, running from the pithead to staiths on the River Wear in Sunderland. Stephenson's scheme consisted of no less than ten components – two sections worked by locomotives, three by fixed cable engines and five self-acting inclined planes. Even with all these complications, Stephenson's option still forecast higher productivity than was predicted from the purely horse-drawn version. By the time it opened, Stephenson had built three locomotives for the company, named *Dart, Tallyho* and *Star*, after local racehorses.

The opening of the railway was a success. These locomotives could pull seventeen loaded wagons, averaging 64 tons, at 4mph. It was later calculated

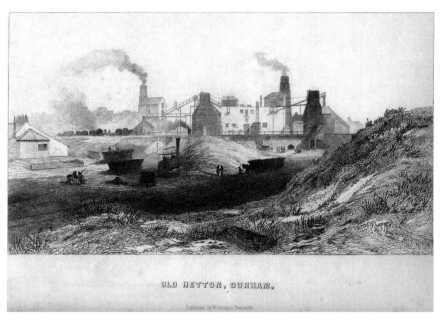

OLD HETTON, DURHAM.

Hetton Colliery pithead, with one of Stephenson's locomotives in the foreground.

that the daily cost of running two locomotives was £2 9s 2d (£2.46). The cost of using horses to do the same work would have been £6.

The Hetton and Killingworth locomotives were much modified over the years, including replacing the steam suspension with steel plate springs, once these could be manufactured to the strength required to support the boiler.

Stockton and Darlington – and *Locomotion*

The promoters of the Stockton and Darlington Railway, which was to become the world's first steam-operated public railway, initially specified a horse-drawn railway in 1818. John Rennie, who had first looked at the route in 1810, had been asked to consider the respective merits of a canal and a tramway. He had favoured a canal, but this scheme was sunk on the grounds of cost, Napoleonic war delays and by the fact that the proposed canal would have bypassed the Pease business premises in Darlington. It was replaced by the proposal for a horse-drawn railway and that is what is shown on the company's corporate seal.

The first bill was vague as to the means of motive power. It offered the options of wagons being drawn by 'men or horses'. The draft bill had included the option of steam power, but many of the legislators in London had no idea what a 'loco-motive' was and the word was struck from the draft. Even so, the first bill was lost in Parliament in 1819.

The promoters of the scheme came back with a second draft bill in April 1821, by which time George Stephenson had replaced George Overton as engineer of the railway. To Overton 'an engine on

The corporate seal of the Stockton and Darlington Railway, showing its original intention to be horse-drawn. What today might be called its mission statement reads 'Private Risk for Public Service'.

the public (rail) road would be a perpetual nuisance', making it ironic that the world's earliest recorded steam railway journey, at Penydarren, was on rails laid by Overton. The change in personnel thus gave an opportunity to review the mode of travel. The second bill was still vague about this, referring to 'men, horses or otherwise', though elsewhere it did allow for 'loco-motive or moveable steam engines'. Even so, it took a further Act of Parliament before the more controversial use of steam power to transport both goods and human passengers was officially approved.

In the end, the railway used a combination of locomotives, stationary steam engines and horse power. In July 1824 the company ordered two locomotives at £600 each from Robert Stephenson and Co., the company set up by the Stephensons and Edward Pease, which was the driving force behind the Stockton and Darlington Railway. On the opening day, the one and only steam locomotive that was by then in service – official title 'the Company's locomotive engine' but later better known as Stephenson's *Locomotion No. 1* – was preceded by a man on horseback. Locomotion became part of the world's first steam-powered passenger railway (though some of the steeper parts had to be worked by stationary steam engines).

The locomotives followed the model used at Killingworth and Hetton, with cylinders set into the top of the boiler and a centre flue boiler, leading to the perennial problem of poor steaming. Extensive use was made of cast iron in its construction, though some parts, like the frame, were timber. It is thought to have been the first locomotive to link its driving wheels together with coupling rods, to give better adhesion when accelerating. The driver perched precariously on a plank alongside the boiler. With the vertical cylinders giving a bouncy ride along relatively rough tracks, simply staying aboard must have been quite an achievement for the driver.

The train *Locomotion* pulled on the opening day was 122m long and 80 tonnes in weight. It was said to have reached up to 24mph (38.6km/h) on parts of that opening day journey but technical problems delayed it, leaving its average journey speed at just 8mph (12.9km/h). *Locomotion's* official maximum speed was given as 15mph (24km/h).

It suffered a boiler explosion in 1828, killing its driver (another one who had tied down the safety valve). It was rebuilt but, as a result of advances in

This replica of Stephenson's *Locomotion* was taking part in a 150th anniversary celebration of the Stockton and Darlington Railway in 1975. (National Railway Museum/Science and Society Picture Library)

railway technology, was obsolete in less than a decade. It was later used as a static engine to pump water out of a west Durham colliery, before being offered for sale as scrap in 1850 at a price of £100. No buyer came forward. It was finally preserved in 1857 and can now be seen at Darlington Railway Centre and Museum.

The locomotives on the Stockton and Darlington were unreliable at first. *Locomotion* broke a wheel almost on the first day and was out of commission until mid October. The wheels were a recurrent problem, and ended up with the original spoked version being replaced by the plug design with which we are now familiar. The second locomotive, *Hope*, was delivered in November 1825, but took a week to get ready for service. Further locomotives were delivered and more problems emerged. In 1827 they acquired the only locomotive ever built by Robert Wilson. Its original official name was *Traveller*, but it was nicknamed *Chittaprat* from the unusual noise it made when running. It was due to go to the Stratford and Moreton Railway, until that line was banned from using steam locomotion. With the Stockton and Darlington it proved to be bad enough to be almost immediately cannibalised for spare parts, from which Timothy Hackworth, the line's Locomotive Superintendent, built the much more successful *Royal George*.

Royal George, Timothy Hackworth's rebuild of a failing locomotive, which gave splendid service on the Stockton and Darlington Railway.

A batch of new locomotives were ordered from Stephensons, but the first one was found on arrival in 1828 to be too heavy and had to be rebuilt with six wheels, as did the rest of the batch. In 1828 the railway suffered a second boiler explosion within four months, again killing the driver. Both were caused by the safety valves being left fixed down while the engine was stationary. It has been claimed that the rebuilding of *Chittaprat* was 'a last experiment' by Hackworth to 'make an engine in his own way'. It has even been suggested that the company would have abandoned locomotives altogether, had it not been for the fact that Edward Pease (the financial and managerial muscle behind the railway) and Thomas Richardson (a senior director of the railway) were both partners in Stephenson's Newcastle locomotive works. Other sources refute this.

Locomotion

Built by Robert Stephenson and Company (1825)
Wheels: 0-4-0 − 48in (1.219m) driving wheels
Boiler pressure: 50psi
Heating surface: 60 sq ft (5.57 sq m)
Cylinders: two of 9.5in by 24in (241mm by 610mm)
Official maximum speed: 15mph (24km/h)
Tractive effort: 1,900ft lb (foot-pounds)★
Working life: 1825 to 1857

★ A foot-pound is a measure of work, based on the energy involved in moving a weight of one pound through a distance of one foot. One horsepower works out at 33,000 ft lb per minute.

Royal George. The fifth locomotive to be purchased by the Stockton and Darlington was officially named *Stockton,* but was nicknamed *Chittaprat* from the distinctive noise it made while in motion. It was built by Robert Wilson of Newcastle. He was not a prolific maker but this example was characterised by having four cylinders, two acting on each pair of wheels, with cranks acting at right angles to each other. It was delivered to the Stockton and Darlington in 1826, but in October of that year was involved in a collision. It had never been a satisfactory locomotive in its original form.

By 1827 Timothy Hackworth, the locomotive superintendent of the Stockton and Darlington was struggling to keep his unreliable fleet of locomotives working, while designing three new ones. The railway's management authorised him to build a locomotive that would 'exceed the efficiency of horses' and he cannibalised the boiler from *Chittaprat* to build *Royal George,* the most successful and powerful locomotive of its time. It had direct drive from its cylinders to the wheels and was the first locomotive to have three axles connected by outside coupling rods. As such, it was the grandfather of a long line of British 0-6-0 goods engines and came into service on 29 November 1827.

It weighed 50 per cent more than the Stephenson-designed locomotives of the day, giving it greater traction, but its six wheels spread the load more evenly, minimising the possibility of rail breakage. It could pull a 30 per cent heavier train than the other (Stephenson-built) locomotives used on the Stockton and Darlington. Among its other features was a properly aligned steam blastpipe, thought to be one of the first locomotives to incorporate this, and copied by the Stephensons in their 1830 updating of *Rocket*. Many – going back to Trevithick – had used versions of the blastpipe, but Hackworth was the first to master the ideal size, location and alignment for it (though, as we will see, he had not quite mastered it in time for his Rainhill trial entrant, *Sans Pareil*). *Royal George* also had an improved boiler, with twice the surface heating area of *Locomotion*.

Royal George cost £425 to build and in 1828 it carried 22,422 tons of coal along the 20-mile line at a cost of £466. This cost included repairs, maintenance and interest on capital. It was estimated that the same work done by horses would have cost £998. It clearly 'exceeded the efficiency of horses', though it was not the first locomotive to do so. Some other engineers were a little sniffy about *Royal George*, saying it was no more than a 'good serviceable engine', that it was slow and the vertical or inclined cylinders of Hackworth engines were an obsolescent feature. But such criticisms missed the point, for *Royal George* was ideal for a single-track line dominated by heavy minerals trains. Speed was not essential – what mattered more were reliability in all weathers and pulling power – and *Royal George* could pull 130 tons of coal at 5mph on a level track.

By contrast, many of Stephenson's earlier locomotives, designed for short colliery runs, were cruelly exposed by the longer journeys under the more arduous conditions that the Stockton and Darlington required. The management of the railway were certainly happy with *Royal George*'s performance, paying Hackworth a bonus of £20 for his handiwork. It remained in service until December 1840, when it was sold to the Wingate Colliery Company, making the Stockton and Darlington a profit of £125 on their original outlay.

Royal George
Rebuilt by Timothy Hackworth (1827)
Wheels: 0-6-0: 4ft (122cm) diameter
Cylinders: 11in by 20in (28cm by 51cm)
Heating surface: 141 sq ft
Normal payload: 24 wagons (100 tons) at 5mph on the flat

Robert Stephenson and Co.'s *Invicta*. George Stephenson was appointed engineer to the Canterbury and Whitstable Railway in 1825 and specified a combination of stationary engines and horse-drawn vehicles to operate this short but hilly line. But the proprietors disagreed with him and insisted on having a locomotive to work the flattest parts of the line. They ordered one from Stephensons: what they got was *Invicta*. This was the twentieth locomotive built by the company and immediately followed *Rocket,* with which it had much in common. One noticeable difference between them was that, while both engines had two cylinders set at an angle, *Invicta*'s drove the rear wheels, rather than the front ones (as on *Rocket*).

Invicta, the Canterbury and Whitstable Railway's unsuccessful locomotive. (CC SA 2.0 via WikimediaCommons)

Invicta cost the railway £635 and was to be part of a dedicated steam-powered passenger service. It arrived in Whitstable and it was soon evident that something was wrong with it. Its lack of power was such that it could not pull a train up the inclined length of track leading out of the town. From 1832 the railway had to install a stationary engine at the top of that incline to pull the trains up. The only length of track *Invicta* could work unaided was a 1-mile relatively flat stretch at South Street.

In 1836 it was decided to carry out some design modifications to improve *Invicta*'s performance. These included the addition of another cylinder ring, the removal of the firebox and the replacement of the multi-tube boiler with a single-flue boiler. This last one is particularly incomprehensible, given that a multi-tube boiler was already widely known to be more efficient than a single flue. Predictably these changes made a bad performance worse, and the locomotive was little used until withdrawn completely from service in 1839. A buyer was sought for it, but none materialised. *Invicta* came into the ownership of the South Eastern Railway in 1844 and was put into store at the Ashford Works, becoming the first locomotive to be preserved for posterity. Over the years it has served as an (unworthy?) symbol of the pioneering days of steam rail travel, and has been trotted out at many commemorations and anniversaries.

Invicta
Built by Robert Stephenson and Company (1829)
Wheels: 2-2-0
Gauge: 4ft 8 in (1.435m)
Driver diameter: 4ft (1.219m)
Weight: 6.4 tons
Boiler pressure: 40psi
Heating surface: 192 sq ft (17.8 sq m)
Cylinders: two of 10.5in by 18in (254mm by 457mm)
Tractive effort: 1,275ft lb

Timothy Hackworth and *Sans Pareil*. Timothy Hackworth had many achievements in his long career as an engine builder, but the one that arguably brought him into greater public attention than any other was one in which he failed – the Rainhill trial of 1829. He decided to submit an entry for the 'most improved engine' competition – quite rightly so, since he was one of a very small number of people in the country at that time who was capable of building a plausible candidate for the title.

His entry was *Sans Pareil*, a French name meaning 'without equal'. He started at a disadvantage to the frontrunners in the contest, the Stephensons, in that he did not have the facilities to manufacture all the parts at his place of work. Some had to be contracted out, which in Hackworth's case meant to the Stephensons. This gave them prior knowledge of at least part of what one of their leading competitors was planning.

A replica of *Sans Pareil* at a recreation of the Rainhill trial. (Barry Lewis/Oxyman CC 2.0 via WikimediaCommons)

Another disadvantage for Hackworth was that some of his technology was less cutting edge than the Stephensons'. First, *Rocket* had one of the first multi-tube boilers, which made steam production much more efficient, whereas *Sans Pareil* had a less effective single-flue tube (albeit in a U shape within the boiler to increase the heating surface area). Second, Hackworth tended to opt for old-fashioned upright cylinders, which gave the locomotive a strange rolling gait as it went along and which would, at higher speeds, have made it distinctly unstable. *Rocket* had at least started the transition towards the horizontal cylinders that are now agreed to be the optimum for a steam locomotive, having its cylinders set at about 45 degrees to the horizontal.

Thirdly, as we saw, Hackworth had not yet mastered the correct design for his blastpipe, with the result that a good part of the engine's fuel was blown out of the chimney, unburnt or worse, still burning. This gave appalling fuel consumption figures, for which *Sans Pareil* would have been marked down by the judges. These points aside, it was a competent locomotive of its day, and the Stephensons regarded it as one of the, if not *the*, best of their rivals.

Sans Pareil had two cylinders, mounted vertically at the opposite end to the chimney. They drove one pair of wheels directly and the other via connecting rods. One problem with this was that it made it impossible for the locomotive to have springs. There was initially some dispute as to whether *Sans Pareil* could take part in the trial, since it was claimed to be overweight, but it was finally admitted, carrying out eight trips at a top speed of just over 16mph. It then had to be retired with various mechanical failures, including a cracked cylinder. Ironically, the cylinder was one of the components the Stephensons had manufactured for Hackworth. There was initially some talk of foul play, but this seems to have been dismissed, since the cracked cylinder was only discovered after it had retired with its other faults.

Sans Pareil was bought by the Liverpool and Manchester Railway, which used it briefly before selling it to John Hargreaves and Son in 1831. It leased it to the Bolton and Leigh Railway for £15 a month, and it was used for freight and passenger services until 1844, the company having meanwhile bought the locomotive for £110. It was then leased to Coppull Colliery, Chorley, where it was used as a stationary engine until 1863. It was presented to what is now the Science Museum in 1864.

Sans Pareil
Built by William Hedley and Timothy Hackworth (1829)
Wheels: 0-4-0
Driving wheel diameter: 54in (1.372m)
Weight: 4.32 tons
Cylinders: two of 7in by 18in (17.8cm by 45.7cm)

Stourbridge Lion. This locomotive was internationally famous, despite having made just a trial run and never having been used for its intended purpose (pulling coal wagons). It was built by the firm of Foster, Rastrick and Company, which were based in Stourbridge, hence the first half of its name; the 'lion' part comes from the face painted on its front by someone in America. It was the first full-sized locomotive to be run in the United States, indeed one of the first to operate anywhere outside the United Kingdom.

The Delaware & Hudson Canal Company was established in 1823 to build and operate canals between New York and the coalfields around Carbondale, Pennsylvania. Railways became of interest to it in 1825, initially in the form of an idea to build a railway between the pitheads and the western end of its canal. The company's chief engineer, John B. Jervis, designed a series of inclines between level but unconnected railways. A former colleague of Jervis, Horatio Allen was sent off to England on a railway research tour, armed with the specifications of locomotives that might be used on the D&H. By July he had ordered four locomotives, three from Foster Rastrick and one – *Pride of Newcastle* – from the Stephenson company.

Stourbridge Lion, the first steam locomotive to run on American soil, is watched by crowds as it completes its first test run. (Painting by Clyde O. DeLand, 1916)

The Stephenson locomotive was completed before any of the Foster Rastricks, and arrived in America two months before *Lion*. However, it did not get test-run because of difficulty in raising steam (or, as some would have it, because the railway was not yet complete). Many Stephenson locomotives had suffered from steaming problems and it may in this case have been compounded: (a) by some ill-judged alterations to the *Pride* to try and solve the problem but that actually made things worse, and (b) by the D&H using anthracite, which can be a difficult coal to use with steam locomotives. It is a very pure form of coal, difficult to light but, once lit, burns fiercely with a very pure and smoke-free flame. It also needs a large firebox to use it to its best advantage.

Lion arrived in New York in mid May 1829. It was assembled in West Point foundry in the city, where it immediately became one of the city's main attractions. Thousands visited it daily to see it being steamed. It was eventually moved to Honesdale, Pennsylvania, where its first official test run took place on 8 August. The locomotive performed well but the track did not. Instead of using metal rails they had wooden ones with metal wearing strips on top. The maximum loading for these was 4 tons, but *Lion* weighed nearly twice that, at 7.5 tons. Moreover the wood had cracked and warped from exposure to the sun. The general opinion among those present (according to the American driver on the day, the aforementioned Horatio Allen) seemed to be that 'the iron monster would either break down the road or that it would leave the track at the curve and plunge into the creek'. The scariest part was crossing a 30ft-high wooden trestle, which the driver elected to take alone, and heroically. As he put it: 'believing that the road would prove safe, and preferring, if we did go down to go down handsomely and without any evidence of timidity, I started with considerable velocity'.

Train and driver survived but it never got into service. *Lion* had one more trial run, then was converted into a stationary engine on the (now largely horse-drawn) railway. None of the three other British locomotives were used, being deemed unsuitable for American railways. By about 1830 American manufacturers were starting to build locomotives more suited to their needs (discussed elsewhere). Attempts to sell these first four were fruitless – two were lost in a fire – and they were eventually cannibalised for their wrought iron and other spare parts until the mid 1840s. Once the historic importance of them was realised, souvenir hunters made the vandalism worse, until virtually all that was left of *Lion* was the boiler. It had gone beyond the point of restoration, but most of the fragments that remain are preserved in the Smithsonian Institution.

The only other locomotive subsequently built by Foster Rastrick was a near copy of *Lion* for the British market. It was called *Agenoria* after a Roman goddess of industry. Its main differences were that it was built to British standard gauge and that it had an enormously long (14ft 4in, or 436.9cm) chimney. This was thought to have been designed to create the correct amount of draught for the firebox. It was also thought to be the first locomotive to use mechanical lubrication for its axles. Unlike *Lion*, *Agenoria* had a relatively long working life, from 1829 to about 1854. It can be seen today in the National Railway Museum, York. For more on John Rastrick see also his entry in this book under locomotive pioneers.

Rastrick's *Agenoria*, sister to *Stourbridge Lion*.

Stourbridge Lion

Built by Foster Rastrick and Company (1829)
Wheels: 0-4-0 – 48in (1.219m) driving wheels
Weight: locomotive 12,000lb (6,400kg), tender 5,800lb (2,600kg)
Firebox: 8 sq ft (0.74 sq m)
Boiler: diameter 48in (1.219m) length 10.5ft (3.2m)
Cylinders: two of 8.5in by 36in (21.6cm by 91.4cm)

3

Some Pioneers

In this chapter we look at some of the people who were active in railway building in the years before 1830.

Timothy Hackworth, locomotive builder (1786–1850), was born in Wylam near Newcastle, the same village where George Stephenson, five years his elder, grew up. He was the son of the foreman blacksmith at Wylam Colliery and left school at 14 to begin a seven-year apprenticeship under his father. John Hackworth was a proud father, saying that his son

> gave early indication of a natural bent and aptitude of mind for mechanical construction and research, and it formed a pleasurable theme of contemplation for the father to mark the studious application of his son to obtain the mastery of mechanical principles, and observe the energy and passionate ardour with which he grasped at a thorough knowledge of his art.

His father never saw him complete his apprenticeship – he died in 1804. But Timothy succeeded to his late father's post when he qualified in 1807. He held it for eight years, during which time he worked with William Hedley of Wylam Colliery, assisting in the manufacture of *Puffing Billy* (though his ideas had moved on by the time he was actually in charge of locomotive building). He eventually left Wylam Colliery because his religious convictions (he was a staunch Methodist) would not allow him to work on the Sabbath. His departure heralded the end of locomotive development at the colliery.

He then moved to Walbottle Colliery for another eight-year stint as foreman smith. During this time he was seconded for a year to George Stephenson's Forth Street works while the Stephensons were away on some of their extended business trips. When George returned he was so impressed with Timothy's role in the business in his absence that Stephenson offered him a half-share of his own interest, but Hackworth declined the offer. He returned to Walbottle in the latter part of 1824, but not to the same post, which his brother Thomas had taken over.

The following comes from the record books of the Stockton and Darlington Railway for 13 May 1825:

> John Dixon reports that he has arranged with Timothy Hackworth to come and settle on the line, particularly to have the superintendence of the permanent and locomotive engines. The preliminary arrangement as regards salary of £150 per annum, the company to find a house, and pay for his house, rent and fire.

This was to be one of the high points of his career, though he may not have recognised it as such at the time. He was faced with the challenging task of keeping the Stockton and Darlington's motley assortment of unreliable locomotives working and helping with the development of new ones, such as his work with the Stephensons on *Locomotion No. 1*. He was said to have been in no small part responsible, through his persistence, for the eventual success of both the company's steam locomotives and the company itself. Among his more notable successes was *Royal George*, which gave the company almost twenty years' exemplary service, before being sold on at a healthy profit. As a later chronicler of the line put it:

> He entered upon the duties of a locomotive engineer under circumstances of great difficulty and discouragement. Skilled artisans were then few in number and difficult to obtain. Machinery for turning and fitting had not been brought to anything like its present perfection and the work was consequently of a rude and imperfect kind; while it was also necessary to construct the early locomotives of slender materials.
>
> J.S. Jeans, 1875

Alongside all this, he found time and resources to build one of the finalists for the Rainhill trial – the *Sans Pareil* (discussed earlier). It made a respectable showing in the first part of the trial but was unable to complete it, due to a cracked cylinder and other problems. The locomotive was nonetheless bought by the Stockton and Darlington Company, and leased out to the Bolton and Leigh Railway, where it remained in service until 1844 – longer than *Rocket* managed in front-line service.

In 1833 he entered a new contract with the Stockton and Darlington, which allowed him to combine his work with developing his own business as a manufacturer of locomotive and stationary steam engines, based in Shildon. By 1840 this latter business became a full-time occupation. Among his clients was the London and Brighton Railway, for whom he built a whole class of twelve passenger express locomotives between 1846 and 1848. He died of typhus in 1850, aged 63.

William James, railway promoter (1771–1837), was born into a well-to-do family in Henley-in-Arden, Warwickshire. After qualifying as a solicitor he went to work in his father's law practice, but a share-price collapse in 1797 forced him to quit the family business and carve out a new career as a land agent. He soon had a practice that included many titled and affluent landowners, and one of James' specialities was advising his clients to realise the mineral wealth of their property holdings. This was the context for him beginning, in about 1799, to propose that they should build railways (such as an early proposal for the Bolton and Leigh Railway (1802–03)). He soon saw that the horse-drawn railways that had been serving collieries for 200 years or more could form the basis of a national system of public transport. Unusually among railway pioneers, he saw the potential for them transporting passengers as well as goods.

He got involved in the birth of the steam age. He met Trevithick, saw his Penydarren locomotive at Merthyr Tydfil in 1803 and is thought to have witnessed the running of *Catch Me Who Can* in London in 1808. During the Napoleonic Wars he lobbied the Prince Regent with an idea for a railway linking the naval dockyards at Chatham and Portsmouth (to be used by civilian traffic during peacetime) and in 1820–21 proposed a Central Junction Railway from Stratford-upon-Avon to Paddington. He met with George Stephenson, and a loose arrangement was agreed between them for the marketing of Stephenson's locomotives which came to nothing. Possible routes for various railways were surveyed, including between Canterbury and Whitstable and Liverpool and Manchester, among many others.

James was overstretching himself and in 1822–23 he was imprisoned for debt; later in 1823 he was declared bankrupt. This, and spells of ill health, prevented him bringing most of his schemes to fruition. Such were the complications of his finances that they occupied the Bankruptcy Commissioners for twenty years and ran up legal bills amounting to hundreds of thousands of pounds in modern-day equivalents. Meanwhile, Stephenson later followed much of James' proposed route between Liverpool and Manchester, but used James' least-favoured route between Canterbury and Whitstable.

Partly because George Stephenson refused to acknowledge him (though son Robert and other leading engineers were much more sympathetic), James received little recognition for his work in his lifetime. One scheme he did see through to completion was the Stratford and Avon Canal, which opened in 1816. His contribution to the cause of railways was only recognised much later. He died of pneumonia early in 1837, following a winter journey by mail coach. James' name can be added to the unnaturally long list of parents who can claim to be the father of the railways.

John Urpeth Rastrick, engineer (1780–1856), was the son of an engineering consultant, and his name crops up at several key points in the early history of steam locomotion. He helped Richard Trevithick develop his ideas for the use of high-pressure steam and revealed to Parliament that he had built *Catch me who can*, the locomotive Trevithick had demonstrated in London in 1808, whilst working with locomotive builder John Hazeldine of Bridgnorth. His partnership with Hazeldine broke up in about 1817. One of his later companies, Foster Rastrick and Co., produced a range of ironwork used, among others, by tramways. He also acted as engineer to the Stratford and Moreton Rail Road Company, a 16-mile horse-drawn railway between Stratford on Avon and Moreton-in-the-Marsh.

He was commissioned by James Walker to review the economics of using either rope haulage or locomotives on the new Liverpool and Manchester Railway. His report came out marginally in favour of rope haulage, but in such a way that it opened the door for the Rainhill trial and the eventual triumph of the locomotive. Rastrick was appointed one of the judges at the Rainhill trial. Foster Rastrick only ever produced four locomotives, three of which were exported to America and one of which – *Stourbridge Lion* – won eternal fame in 1829 as the first full-sized locomotive to run on American soil (discussed in more detail elsewhere in the book). The one surviving example of the four – named *Agenoria* – is now part of the National Railway Museum's collection in York. His locomotives have been described as direct descendants of the *Puffing Billy*-type, with a great deal of improvement and simplification (including the first example of mechanical lubrication).

After the dissolution of the Foster Rastrick Company, John became an independent civil engineer, working on many projects. These included, in 1835, helping John Rennie the Younger to secure Parliamentary approval for the London and Brighton Railway, whose construction he then oversaw as consultant engineer. It was only one of a number of railway-related schemes he undertook, including the Brighton and Chichester and the Brighton, Lewes and Hastings Railways. He also designed and/or built many viaducts, tunnels and bridges.

Edward Bury, locomotive builder (1794–1858), was born in Salford, the son of a timber merchant. By 1826 he had set himself up as an iron founder and locomotive engineer. He started out at premises at Tabley Street, Liverpool, near the Liverpool and Manchester Railway's workshops. He hoped from there to sell locomotives to the railway, but he was in competition with George Stephenson, who thwarted his plans. He only ever sold one locomotive – called *Liver* and dating from 1832 – to the Liverpool and Manchester Railway.

After this rebuttal Bury moved to new premises and started to build his first locomotive. *Dreadnaught* was an 0-6-0, and was intended as an entry in the Rainhill trial, but could not be completed in time to compete. Furthermore, the Liverpool and Manchester then declined to buy it, apparently because it had six wheels. It was sold to the Bolton and Leigh railway in 1831, as was the second Bury engine, *Liverpool*. This time, the

Liverpool and Manchester's reason for not buying it was the size of its four coupled wheels (6ft, which Stephenson said was 'dangerous' and they were later reduced to 4ft 6in).

But *Liverpool* was an advanced and efficient design, which paved the way for most of Bury's subsequent output, with near horizontal cylinders, a multi-tube boiler, a round dome-shaped firebox and a wrought-iron frame inside the wheels. It was a package that was widely copied, both here and abroad. Bury had greater luck selling to other railway companies.

In 1836 he became the Contractor for Locomotive Power on the new London and Birmingham Railway, a post he held until 1846, and for whom he built half its original ninety engines. According to Dendy Marshall, he handicapped the company by insisting on using four-wheeled locomotives throughout this period. He said that they were less costly than six-wheelers, took up less space, were lighter and safer and adapted themselves better to the rails. His views were the subject of lively debate between 1832 and 1854 but, as Stretton put it, 'ultimately Mr Bury's "four-wheeled theory" was proved to be erroneous'.

As an aside, the Stephensons became early converts to an alternative six-wheeled approach; having used them successfully on goods locomotives, they applied the same approach to their Patentee class of passenger engines, supplied to the Liverpool and Manchester Railway from 1834. One of their features, from a Stephenson patent of 1833, was that six-wheeled engines should not have flanges on the middle set of wheels, making it easier for them to pass around tight curves. The Patentee class became influential and widely copied, both at home and abroad.

This difference of opinion between Bury and Stephenson led to a proposed trial of strength in 1833. The Leicester and Swannington Railway had bought its first six engines from Stephenson and Co., but some of its directors wanted to give a trial to Bury's rival engine, *Liver*. They sought informal advice from George Stephenson, who suggested a tug-of-war between the two rival engines to see which was superior. Stephenson put up his six-coupled-wheel *Atlas* as his candidate. Some tests with trains of wagons were set up on the Swannington Railway but, before it got to a tug-of-war, Bury had to admit that his engine could not cope with the size of trains pulled by *Atlas*. When built, *Atlas* was the largest, heaviest and most powerful locomotive running.

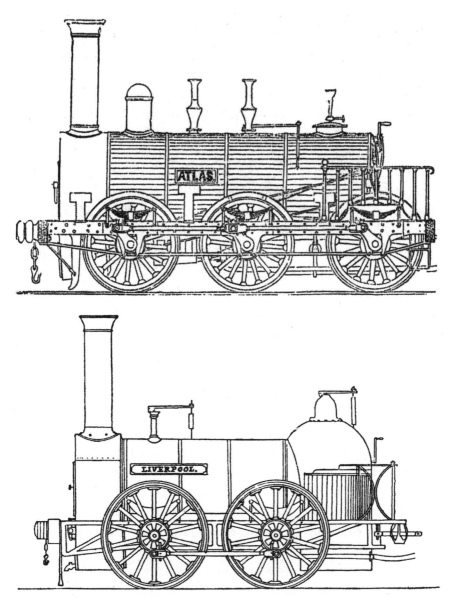

The rivals: Stephenson's *Atlas* and Bury's *Liverpool*. *Atlas'* six-wheeled drive trumped *Liverpool*'s four.

Bury exported many of his locomotives and also built engines for boats. His first four-wheeled inside-cylinder engine was commenced in January 1831. In England it was known as *Liverpool*, but it was exported to the St Petersburg Railroad in America, where it was renamed *Spitfire*. In 1848 Bury became

locomotive engineer on the Great Northern Railway and the following year its general manager. He advised on the building of three railway
towns – Doncaster, Swindon and Wolverton, and in later years was show-
ered with honorific titles, including Fellowships of the Royal Society, the
Royal Astronomical Society and the Royal Historical Society, and mem-
berships of the Smeatonian Society of Civil Engineers and the Institution
of Civil Engineers.

Henry Booth, railway promoter (1788–1869), was the son of a
Liverpool corn merchant. He followed in his father's line of business
until 1822, when the scheme to build a railway between Manchester and
Liverpool went public. He became one of its strongest supporters, writing the railway's prospectus and becoming the secretary to the committee.
Once the scheme was approved by Parliament he was made a managing
director, company secretary and treasurer – effectively its chief executive.
He played a large part in ensuring that locomotive steam was the motive
power chosen for the railway, and that his friend, George Stephenson, was
successful in the Rainhill trial.

He had considerable mechanical skills and was behind the sugges-
tion that the *Rocket* should employ a version of the multi-tube boiler,
recently reinvented by the French railway pioneer Marc Seguin. This was
one of the very first uses of the boiler, which before long would become
standard equipment on steam locomotives, and it did much to resolve the
perennial problem of inadequate steaming experienced by many early
Stephenson locomotives. He was also responsible for other innovations,
such as screw couplings and spring buffers, which are still part of railway
operation today.

He saw the Liverpool and Manchester Railway through Parliamentary
approval, construction and into operation. In 1846 various companies
merged to form the London and North Western Railway Company, and
Booth was appointed secretary for the northern section, later becoming one of its overall directors. He remained with the company until his
retirement in 1859, whereupon his fellow directors gave him a gratuity of
5,000 guineas (£5,250) – a substantial amount for the day – for a lifetime
of loyal service. He remained active in public life in retirement, both as a
magistrate and in support of the liberal causes he espoused.

Joseph Locke, railway builder (1805–60), was born in Sheffield, the son of a mining engineer. By the age of 17 he had already served apprenticeships under William Stobart on the south side of the Tyne and under his father. He went to work for the Stephensons at their Forth Street locomotive works, where they were building locomotives for the Stockton and Darlington railway. Locke and Robert Stephenson became close friends and Locke, despite his youth, took on considerable responsibility within the works.

While the management of the Liverpool and Manchester were trying to make up their minds about the choice of motive power for the railway, Locke was the co-author with Robert Stephenson of a report extolling the advantages of steam locomotion. The report played into the hands of Henry Booth and other pro-locomotive members of the board, enabling them to propose the Rainhill trial and leading to the eventual victory of *Rocket*.

When the Liverpool and Manchester Bill was thrown out by Parliament, the route was resurveyed by Charles Vignoles. In addition, Locke was asked to resurvey the tunnelling works needed for the railway, in particular those already undertaken. Locke was heavily critical of the latter, which reflected badly on George Stephenson and created a tension between the two. Even so, when the Liverpool and Manchester was finally approved and George Stephenson reinstated, he appointed Locke as one of his assistant engineers for the project , with Vignoles as the other. Vignoles and Stephenson soon fell out and Locke was left as the only assistant. Locke took over responsibility for the western part of the route. Perhaps the biggest challenge facing them was the crossing of the bog at Chat Moss. Stephenson usually gets the credit for this imaginative feat of engineering, but it has been suggested that the idea was actually Locke's.

On the opening day of the Liverpool and Manchester Railway, eight trains carried the invited guests. Locke was at the controls of *Rocket* (but not to blame) when it struck and killed the Parliamentarian William Huskisson.

In 1829 George Stephenson was appointed engineer of the Grand Junction Railway, linking the Liverpool and Manchester line with Birmingham. Once again he chose Locke as his assistant. The experience of the Liverpool and Manchester had thrown Stephenson's lack of ability in organising major engineering projects into sharp relief, whereas Locke was highly skilled at it. The railway management decided to make Locke responsible for the northern half of the new line, with Stephenson looking after the southern part. Once again, Stephenson's shortcomings, and Locke's skill, soon became apparent. Locke had all the contracts for his part of the line in place before Stephenson had signed a single one. When the railway company tried to make the two of them joint chief engineers Stephenson solved the problem by resigning in protest. Locke was left in sole charge, leading to a further rift between the two of them and even his son Robert Stephenson's friendship with Locke being put under duress.

Rather than breaking the Grand Junction project down into a lot of small contracts, Locke had just a few large ones, working with contractors he knew and trusted. Locke delivered the 80-mile railway by July 1837 and with very little overrun on his initial estimate (the final cost was £18,846 per mile, compared with Locke's estimated £17,000). Robert Stephenson could not claim the same for his London to Birmingham line, nor Brunel for his Great Western.

The Lancaster and Carlisle Railway highlighted another difference in approach. The Stephensons had little faith in the hill-climbing abilities of early locomotives, and would go miles out of their way to avoid steep slopes. Locke had far more confidence in the new technology. George Stephenson's 1839 survey route from Lancaster to Carlisle avoided the hilly Lake District altogether by going round it. The railway company rejected this route and instead went for a much more direct but challenging route over Shap Fell, surveyed by Locke. It was a challenging route for trains (as it still is today) but it worked, and saved time and money. There was a similar difference of opinion between them, and a similar outcome, over the route from Carlisle to Glasgow.

Locke built many other major railways, including about three-quarters of the West Coast Main Line to Scotland. He also advised Parliament about many of the major railway issues of the day, such as Brunel's atmospheric railway (which he opposed) and the gauge commissioners (where he and Robert Stephenson were successful in securing a standardisation – outside of Great Western territory – on the 4ft 8½in standard gauge). He was also President of the Institution of Civil Engineers and a Member of Parliament for Honiton, Devon, from 1847.

Edward Pease, railway promoter (1767–1858), was part of a family of Quakers engaged in the woollen industry in Yorkshire. The family were held in high public esteem and were persuaded by their customers to open a bank for the safekeeping of their money. The Pease Partners Bank, opened in Hull in 1754, was the first of its kind in Yorkshire. Travelling around the county, Pease saw the changes taking place in the iron and coal industries and became convinced of the need for a railway to carry coal from the pits to navigable water and thence to its markets in London and elsewhere. As

Edward Pease, the man behind the Stockton and Darlington Railway. (*Illustrated London News*)

we saw, an initial feasibility study for the Stockton and Darlington was carried out by John Rennie as early as 1810. He considered the respective merits of a canal or a horse-drawn tramway. Rennie opted for the canal, but this was rejected, partly on the grounds that his route completely bypassed Darlington.

The scheme was eventually approved by Parliament in 1821, but Pease's ideas until that time were fixed on a horse-drawn railway. Then he met George Stephenson and was persuaded by him that the future lay in steam locomotion. The Pease family put up much of the money to pay for the construction of the railway and locomotives (Pease became a major shareholder in Robert Stephenson and Company, locomotive engineers) and (as further Parliamentary permission was granted) the Stockton and Darlington became the world's first public steam railway. While Pease gave George Stephenson his big chance, he was not unreserved in his view of Stephenson's management skills by the conclusion of the Stockton and Darlington contract. Nonetheless, Pease and fellow director Thomas Richardson did such a good job of singing Stephenson's praises during the early days of their relationship that he ended up being engineer for six other major projects, and heavily over-committed. Pease said of Stephenson in 1824 'while his talent and ingenuity is great, his execution is torpid, defective and languid'.

Edward's son, Joseph, became Britain's first Quaker MP in 1832, once the Reform Act of that year removed the requirement for members to swear an oath as a condition of taking up public office. Joseph had been responsible, aged 19, for drawing up the prospectus to help persuade other investors that the railway was a sound business proposition.

Charles Vignoles, railway engineer (1793–1875), had a colourful infancy, which included his being taken prisoner of war by the French in the West Indies. From 1825 he was employed by the Rennies on the proposed railway to Brighton, and in resurveying the Liverpool to Manchester line after its initial rejection by Parliament. He assisted John Braithwaite and John Ericsson with their entry *Novelty* for the Rainhill trial.

By the early 1830s he had established a reputation as one of the country's leading railway engineers, working on the North Union Railway between Wigan and Preston, as well as projects in Ireland, France and (what would become) Germany. In the Sheffield, Ashton-under-Lyne and Manchester railway (1835–40) he faced the challenge of building the longest tunnel then projected in Britain (the original Woodhead tunnel) though the duration of his involvement with this was short, due to financial differences.

At the same time, he worked on improvements to the rail infrastructure, introducing in 1837 the flat-bottomed Vignoles rail that is now almost universal on continental railways. He also found time in 1841 to become the first Professor of Civil Engineering at University College.

The years of railway mania saw him fully employed, including the East Kent line (later known as the London, Chatham and Dover Railway) and further lines in Ireland, Switzerland and particularly Russia, where he employed a large staff. In the 1850s he extended his work to Brazil, the Basque provinces of Spain and Poland. He was also a member of the Institution of Civil Engineers (1827) and its President

Charles Blacker Vignoles, railway builder.

(1869), a fellow of the Royal Astronomical Society (1829) and a fellow of the Royal Society (1855).

But he could also be a most uncivil engineer, given to violently temperamental outbursts when things went wrong. He would indulge in wild gestures, foot-stamping, hair tearing (his own) and a tirade of foul language most unbecoming in a president of an institution.

Benjamin Outram, tramway pioneer (1764–1805), was the son of Joseph Outram, a promoter of the Cromford Canal (from Cromford to the Erewash canal basin in Derbyshire). William Jessop was employed to design and build it, and he recruited Joseph's 24-year-old son Benjamin as his assistant. The construction works, and in particular the 2,966-yard-long Butterley Tunnel, revealed rich deposits of minerals and when the Butterley estate came up for sale the canal company's solicitor, Francis Beresford, bought it. He helped Outram to acquire a 50 per cent holding in it, and thus was born the ironworks of Benjamin Outram & Company in 1790. Outram became a leading advocate of tramways (or, as he always called them, railways) using L-section rails, and his company manufactured both the rails and the wagons to run on them. The first tramway he built ran for just over a mile, from his own quarry at Crich to the Cromford Canal.

He combined his interest in tramways with extensive work on canal building, sometimes combining the two by building railways to serve canals. In the case of the Somerset Coal Canal Company, he took integration one step further, recommending that the canal boats carry their coal in containers that could be lifted by cranes onto and from the wagons on the tramway. He also built Britain's first iron aqueduct, to cross the River Derwent at Nottingham in 1796. But he always saw railways superseding canals within a few years of their construction. He was an early advocate of a standard gauge for all railways, writing in 1799 that 'it seems desirable that all extensive railways should be of the same width and that width should be sufficient to suit all the purposes of trade'. Many of his tramways were built to a 4ft 2in (1.260cm) gauge.

After Benjamin's premature death in 1805 (at the age of 41) he left no will and his family were reduced to poverty for a time, as the courts squabbled over his estate. But his company continued, changing its name in 1809 to the Butterley Company. It became one of the largest and most prestigious ironworks in Britain, specialising in structural steelwork and railway equipment.

Opinions about Outram the man seem to be somewhat divided. A letter of 1805 describes him as 'a fine-looking high-spirited man, of a generous temper and a relentless energy which would ill-brook opposition'. But his wife said he was 'hasty in his temper, feeling his own superiority over others. Accustomed to command, he had little toleration for stupidity or slowness, and none for meanness or littleness of any kind.'

Joseph Sandars, railway promoter (1785–1860), was a wealthy Liverpool-based corn merchant, whose main claim to railway fame was his promotion of the Liverpool and Manchester Railway. He had been unhappy with the speed and cost of moving goods between Liverpool and Manchester, when he met railway promoter William James and was persuaded by him of the need for a railway between the two towns. James was engaged to survey the route but failed to deliver and in 1824 was replaced as engineer by George Stephenson.

Sandars played a leading role in drawing up the railway's prospectus and bringing together a committee of the great and the good to drive the scheme forward. Sandars was a deputy chairman and a director and, on the opening day of the railway, drove the locomotive *Dart*. Sandars retained his interest in the railway after it merged into the Grand Junction Railway in 1845 and then merged again, into the London and North Western Railway in 1846.

Among his other claims to fame, in 1819 he bought the thirty-seven works of art that would eventually form the nucleus of the city's Walker Art Gallery.

Thomas Gray, advocate of railways (1778–1848), was born in Leeds, and spent much of his adult life promoting the cause of railway networks for the United Kingdom and Europe. In 1820 he published *Observations on a General Iron Railway,* (the full title of the book continues) *or Land-Steam Conveyance: to Supersede the Necessity of Horses in all Public Vehicles; Showing its Vast Superiority in Every Respect, over All the Present Pitiful methods* *of Conveyance by Turnpike Roads, Canals and Coasting Traders. Containing every Species of Information Relative to Railroads and Locomotive Engines.* The book went through several editions between then and 1825 and was translated into French and German.

He was a contemporary of the Stephensons, Brunel and William James and was thought to have been influential over them and other pioneers. His central thesis was that there should be a general (i.e. national) passenger railway, funded jointly by the Government and the private sector and directed to 'the good of the Community'. In the event, the Government (who were not among those influenced by him) allowed the British network to be built on a more or less purely free-market basis. The Belgian model for developing railways (described elsewhere in the book) is closer to Gray's ideal, and there is a street in Brussels, where he lived for some time, named after him. Among his other proposals was a rack railway between London and Edinburgh.

William Jessop, civil engineer (1745–1814), was known mainly for his canal and harbour works, though he was involved in some important railway schemes. He was the engineer to the Surrey Iron Railway (discussed elsewhere in the book), which was to have been the first stage of a major railway between London and Portsmouth) and its extension to Croydon and Merstham. He was an early advocate for a tramway between Liverpool and Manchester, and was also engineer to the Kilmarnock and Troon Railway (built 1807–12). This had a number of Scottish firsts: the first railway in Scotland to receive Parliamentary approval; the first to use a steam locomotive and the first to carry passengers. The line also carried coal from the mines around Kilmarnock to the port of Troon. It was a successful line, despite overrunning its construction budget of £38,167 by 52 per cent and its use of steam locomotion not being exactly unblemished (it wrecked the fragile cast-iron plateway tracks). More generally, it seems Jessop was not always spot-on with his estimates; on another scheme, the Leicester Navigation, his initial estimate of £43,166 turned into a final cost of about £96,000.

Nicholas Wood, colliery and locomotive engineer (1795–1865), was born in Ryton, County Durham, the son of another Nicholas and Ann.

Nicholas Senior was the mining engineer at Crawcrook Colliery. Nicholas Junior started his career at Killingworth Colliery. By 1815, Wood had become the viewer or manager of the colliery, where he developed a close working relationship with the colliery engine-wright, one George Stephenson. Among other joint contributions he helped Stephenson with the revolutionary design of his miners' safety helmet and with the design of the early Stephenson locomotive *Blucher*. Stephenson even sent his son Robert to Wood to serve his apprenticeship, where he flourished.

Wood and George Stephenson went together to a momentous meeting with Edward Pease in Darlington, where Pease was persuaded to abandon plans for a horse-hauled Stockton and Darlington Railway in favour of steam power, with George Stephenson in charge of its construction. By 1825 his reputation was such that he published an influential book, *A Practical Treatise on Rail Roads and Interior Communication*, and in 1829 was appointed one of the judges at the Rainhill trials.

In later years he was involved in many good works. He was a frequent advisor to both Houses of Parliament (including on the Liverpool and Manchester Railway Bill). He founded the bodies that were to become the core of Newcastle University. In the wake of a major mining disaster where fifty lives were lost, he helped found what was to become the North of England Institute of Mining and Mechanical Engineers, of which he would become the inaugural and lifetime president.

With railways he was involved in building the Newcastle and Carlisle Railway and was a director of the Newcastle and Berwick Railway. In 1864 he was made a Fellow of the Royal Society and his four sons all made names for themselves through their family's coal-industry-related expertise, one becoming an MP and another a Baronet.

4

Rainhill

As the plans for the construction of the Liverpool and Manchester railway got under way, the promoters had some choices to make. Did they follow the Stockton and Darlington's example and operate a turnpike-type system, open to all users (with all the chaos that could entail) or did they break with the orthodoxy of the day and seek to become a monopolistic common carrier, controlling all the services using their lines?

Then there was the question of what rates they should charge for their services? One of the charging categories they chose was 'Persons, Cattle and other Animals'. This was one of the first official confirmations that railway passengers were to be treated like cattle, and certainly not the only one. The Sheffield, Ashton and Manchester Railway ordered their first cattle trucks in 1845, specifying that they should be 'fitted with spring buffers and drawbars, to answer occasionally for passengers'. On the Radstock line in Somerset, each market day from 1815 the coal trucks would be swept out, boards placed across them to serve as seats and local people would thus be chauffeured to Radstock market.

But most of all there was confusion in the minds of the Liverpool and Manchester board as to what the motive power on their railway should be. One group favoured steam locomotive engines, but their leading light, George Stephenson, stood likely to gain from any such decision (not least because at that time his son's company was just about the only active loco-motive manufacturer in the country) and his impartiality was in doubt. Other board members favoured the tried and tested means of stationary steam engines or horses. Locomotives were, in their view, still at the developmental stage.

Other factors preventing this decision from being a foregone conclusion in favour of locomotives were that tracks for steam locomotives were more expensive to buy and maintain than those for horses, that locomotives had difficulty coping with frosty or extreme wet weather, and that locomotives were regarded by the public as 'scary' and likely to blow up. This last concern was not helped by the fact that the Stockton and Darlington's first two locomotives suffered fatal boiler explosions in 1828. The resolution of this dilemma would lead to the most important formal trial steam locomotion would face in its entire history.

The board engaged two independent engineers – John Rastrick of Stourbridge and James Walker of Limehouse, London – to investigate the alternatives and make a recommendation. This they did during February 1829, after deputations visited steam locomotives at work in Darlington, Shildon and Newcastle. Whilst acknowledging the potential of locomotives (they spoke of 'expecting improvements in the construction and work of locomotives'), they opted (narrowly and based on then current technology) for a stationary engine system.

This prompted Robert Stephenson and Joseph Locke, the latter a distinguished civil engineer, to produce an alternative assessment, strongly in favour of locomotives, titled *Observations on the comparative merits of locomotive and fixed engines*. They pointed out that nearly twenty stationary engines would be needed, at intervals of a mile and a half. About 150 men would be needed to run and maintain the system and it would be impossible to have sidings or branch lines. Moreover, a single breakdown anywhere within the system would bring the entire railway to a halt.

There seemed to be an impasse until railway directors James Walker and Richard Harrison suggested that there should be a locomotive trial. This would offer a prize (£500, equivalent to £40,379 today) for a 'Locomotive engine which shall be a decided improvement on those now in use'. The sword of Damocles hanging over all the entrants was that, if none of the contestants met the competition criteria and were not a 'decided improvement', the railway would go ahead with stationary engines working the line for its entire length.

Detailed rules for the contest were drawn up. Eight requirements were laid down; they included that the locomotives had to be mounted on springs and weigh not more than 6 tons (with water) if carried on six wheels, or not more than 4½ tons if carried on four wheels. This weight criterion alone effectively ruled out most if not all of the existing locomotives then in operation – Stephenson's *Locomotion* weighed in at about 8 tons, for example. Another important criterion was that:

> The engine, if it weighs six tons, must be capable of drawing after it, day by day, on a well-constructed railway, on a level plane, a train of carriages of the gross weight of twenty tons, including the tender and water tank, at a rate of ten miles an hour, with a pressure of steam on the boiler not exceeding fifty pounds per square inch, though the company reserved the right to test the boiler up to 150psi.

For lighter locomotives, the load was reduced in proportion, to be three times the locomotive's weight.

This early engraving illustrates the carnival atmosphere that prevailed at the Rainhill trials.

Some thought the test criteria were insane; one eminent gentleman from Liverpool thought it impossible for a locomotive ever to travel at 10 miles an hour and declared that, should it ever be done, 'he would undertake to eat a stewed engine wheel for breakfast'. In order to be good neighbours, and safe, the competitors were also required to consume their own smoke (which meant firing them with coke) and to have two safety valves (one beyond the reach of anyone who might try to clamp it shut).

STEPHENSONS 'ROCKET' BUILT 1829.

Rocket, the winner of the Rainhill trial.

Rocket

The competition, which was announced at the end of April 1829, was to be held in October, giving the contestants just six months to prepare. None of Stephenson's existing locomotives – indeed, no engine hitherto built – could meet all the competition requirements, so his company devoted itself to building one that would. *Rocket* was designed specifically to win the Rainhill trial. The Stephensons, assisted by Henry Booth, the railway's pro-locomotive secretary and treasurer, drew upon every bit of performance-enhancing locomotive expertise currently available to them. They knew that the rules called for a locomotive that was fast and light, but which only needed to have moderate pulling power. Going for a single pair of driving wheels was one way of saving a lot of weight.

One problem they had to address was the perennial one of their loco motives' inadequate steaming. It was Booth who came up with the solution. If two wide fire tubes through the boiler exposed a larger surface area to the heat than one, and thereby gave more efficient steaming, why not have a larger number of smaller tubes to further increase the heating area?

It was not a new idea. Matthew Boulton had come up with something similar for a stationary engine in about 1784; James Neville had patented it for a boiler with vertical fire tubes in 1826;' and the French railway pioneer Marc Seguin had patented it for locomotives in 1827 (but only in France, and there is no evidence that Booth or the Stephensons knew of Seguin's patent). The Stephenson's approach on their 'premium engine', having twenty-five fire tubes piercing either end of the boiler, posed some challenging manufacturing difficulties, but they proved to be equal to them. Another competitor, *Novelty*, also tried to increase its fire-tube area by having a single tube, folded in three, but this increased its length disproportionally and so gave a poor draught on the fire. It also made fire-tube cleaning impractical.

Rocket also had an improved design of blastpipe. Stephenson had used blastpipes on his locomotives since 1814 and Trevithick had done so for many years before him. Hackworth also had a blastpipe on his entry, *Sans Pareil*, but, as we will see, it was too enthusiastic for its own good.

The separate firebox on *Rocket* was designed to improve the efficiency of steaming. So *Rocket* could turn cold water into running pressure steam in just an hour.

As we have seen, *Rocket*'s two cylinders were set at an angle to the horizontal, whereas most previous designs had vertical cylinders. Vertical cylinders caused the locomotive to sway as it went along. This new arrangement reduced that swaying effect, and *Rocket* was later modified to have its cylinders set as close as possible to the horizontal, which became the model for subsequent generations of locomotives. The new cylinder arrangement also made it possible for the pistons to be connected directly (and more efficiently) to the driving wheels.

Rocket was designed to meet the strict and somewhat unrealistic criteria of the Rainhill trials, so it should not be a surprise that its record in everyday service was rather less sparkling. Almost from day one it struggled with heavy loads, and its inadequacy was thrown into sharp relief when

the Stephensons launched new and improved models within months of
the railway opening. Locomotive technology was changing rapidly. Its
inclined cylinders, which had seemed a great advance over most previous
locomotives in 1829, had been overtaken within months by the modified
Rocket-type locomotives with horizontal cylinders that were subsequently being delivered to the railway.

Between 1836 and 1840 *Rocket* was relegated to local services on
Lord Carlisle's Railway in Cumbria. Prior even to that it was used as
a mobile test bed for a new type of rotary steam engine (which was
itself a failure). Thereafter it was working on a mineral railway at
Brampton, Cumbria until 1862, when it was donated to what is now the
Science Museum.

Rocket has been much modified over the years and the version now
owned by the Science Museum bears only a superficial resemblance to the
locomotive that triumphed at Rainhill.

Rocket
Built by Robert Stephenson and Company (1829)
Wheels: 0-2-2 – 4ft 8½in (143.5cm) driving wheels
Axle load: 5,850lb (2.65 tonnes)
Weight: 9,500lb (4.4 tonnes)
Boiler pressure: 50psi
Cylinders: two of 8in by 17in (20.3cm by 42.3cm)
Official maximum speed: 30mph (48km/h)
Working life: 1829 to 1862

The public warmed to the prospect of the trial and flocked to Rainhill
in large numbers on 6 October 1829. As well as 10,000 to 15,000 ordinary members of the public, the event was attended by correspondents
of the London newspapers and the engineers for several American railways. Several hundred temporary railway constables had been hired for
the event to keep the crowds in order and off the tracks. Early railways
would all have their own police forces, among other things to deal with
trespass and criminal damage, as well as acting as human signals to the
oncoming trains. Often the railway police forces would pre-date those
of the areas through which they ran (for the first-ever professional police

force – the Metropolitan – was only founded in the same year as the Rainhill trials).

A flat straight route 1½ miles long was marked out along the track, between Whiston and Sutton. Supplies of coal and water were laid on and a blacksmith's shop and a weighing machine had been installed at one end of the test track. There was even a grandstand erected at the mid point. This was more than filled by the thousands of onlookers. Judges had been appointed – John Rastrick, Nicholas Wood (a mining engineer with loco-motive design experience and, coincidentally, a former colleague and close collaborator with George Stephenson) and John Kennedy (a Manchester cotton manufacturer and inventor). The trials were due to last a week; this was longer than expected, due to the need to carry out repairs to two of the competitors.

Rocket's rivals

There was no shortage of submissions for the prize, but most were suf-ficiently fanciful (not to say lunatic) to be quickly disregarded. Only five entries made it to the final stage – possibly a reflection of how few people there were at this time capable of building a working locomotive (or was it that that a possible £500 prize was not sufficient incentive to offset the risk and cost of trying to build a revolutionary locomotive; a third possi-bility was that the promoters did not allow people enough time to prepare their locomotives).

One of the Stephensons' rival entrants for the trial was Timothy Hackworth, foreman blacksmith at Wylam Colliery, and his locomotive, *Sans Pareil,* built on a shoestring at his place of work. It was a smaller version of his acclaimed *Royal George,* a locomotive on the Stockton and Darlington Railway that surpassed anything the Stephensons had provided for it. As we saw, lacking the facilities at Wylam, Hackworth had to get parts of his locomotive made by the Stephensons, giving them prior knowledge of aspects of their rival's design. One of the parts that Stephensons made for Hackworth (one of the cylinders) broke after eight trips, putting paid to any chance it may have had. But the cracked cylinder was only spotted after its withdrawal. The real causes of its withdrawal were a leaking boiler and a faulty feed pump, and these were to some extent self-inflicted. When Hackworth discovered the leak in his boiler he tried the boilerman's time-honoured short-term fix for such a problem – putting oatmeal in the boiler. But this had the effect of clogging up his feeder pipe to the pump with porridge.

Certainly the Stephensons had rated *Sans Pareil*'s chances highly before the trial, but its excessive weight (over 4¾ tons for a four-wheeled locomotive) excluded it from winning the prize (though they were still allowed to compete). It also had problems with boiler leakage and an alarming habit of showering nearby spectators with burning coke, due to an overactive blastpipe. The judges found that its fuel consumption was more than three times that of *Rocket* as a result. It may also help to explain the 5mph speed limit imposed on Hackworth's Stockton and Darlington locomotives in everyday service, when passing through wooded areas of that railway, to minimise the risk of them setting fire to the surrounding countryside.

Sans Pareil was later bought by the Liverpool and Manchester Railway and used briefly by the company, before transferring it to the Bolton and Leigh railway, where it worked until 1844. It was then used as a fixed engine at the Coppull Colliery, near Chorley, Lancashire. After a spell at the Science Museum it was moved to the National Railway Museum, York, where it remains to this day.

Another of the candidates, **Timothy Burstall**, got an early sight of what the Stephensons were doing by simply walking into their premises unannounced and having a look around. Whatever he learned before being shown the door, it did him little good. His locomotive, *Perseverance*, was damaged en route to Rainhill, when the delivery wagon overturned. He spent the first five days of the trial trying to fix it. He got it working by the sixth and final day, but it would do no more than 6mph and the owner, having seen the opposition in action, withdrew it. He was given a £25 consolation prize by the organisers.

A further rival, and early popular favourite, was *Novelty,* built by a Swede and his English partner, **John Ericsson** and **John Braithwaite**, who were better known for their work with building steam-powered fire engines and other inventions. Braithwaite was a distinguished engineer and Ericsson could lay claim to the title of Sweden's greatest scientist.

Novelty had to be built very quickly, since the company only found out about the 'steam race' seven weeks before the event, leading to speculation that *Novelty* was, indeed, a converted fire engine. Certainly it looked rather like one of their fire engines. It was brought to Rainhill without time to test it properly (not least because there were no suitable railways on which to run it near London). Once at the trial they received some assistance from experienced railway engineers Charles Vignoles and Timothy Hackworth. It was relatively tiny, weighing in at 2.2 tonnes, barely half the permitted maximum weight for entrants. *Novelty* had several interesting features. It had an S-shaped tube inside the boiler, which was impossible to clean, and a forced draught from a mechanical blower, going into the ashbox below the fire. It is regarded as being the first tank engine, since it had no tender, but carried its water in a tank slung between the wheels.

Novelty, one of the finalists in the Rainhill trial.

It attracted public interest at the trial when, in a preliminary unloaded run, it briefly achieved the unprecedented speed of 28mph. But it proved unreliable (when a furnace blowback led to an explosion while pulling a load of just 7 tons, leading to its withdrawal). It was also unable to generate adequate steam to deal with heavy trains. As George Stephenson put it: 'Her's got nae goots,' while one of the judges likened her boiler to 'a glorified domestic copper'. But while it was running, it won the hearts of the watching masses, as this from the *Liverpool Mercury* shows:

> It seemed, indeed, to fly, presenting one of the most sublime spectacles of human ingenuity and human daring the world has ever beheld. It actually made one giddy to look at it, and filled thousands with lively fears for the safety of the individuals who were on it, and who seemed not to run along the earth, but to fly, as it were, on the 'wings of the wind'. It is a most sublime sight; a sight, indeed, which the individuals who beheld it will not soon forget.
>
> *Liverpool Mercury*, 9 October 1829

The following December, a fully repaired *Novelty* made some further runs along the course at Rainhill, where it equalled or surpassed some of the performances at the trial by *Rocket*. (In these later trials it apparently reached 60mph at one stage.) Unfortunately for them, they were too late to win any prizes, though the railway company did at least buy *Novelty*. Meanwhile, *Rocket* was doing much to advance the cause of locomotion by giving rides to the movers and shakers of public opinion, pending the opening of the railway.

The final entry to the trial was made by one of the members of the Railway's board, **Thomas Shaw Brandreth**. The *Cyclopede* consisted of two horses placed side by side on a treadmill mounted on a light cart, which drove the vehicle along. Clearly it could not comply with the requirements of the trial (it managed just 5mph, then broke and was the first competitor to be withdrawn). Quite why the *Cyclopede* was included in the final reckoning at all was something of a mystery. Was it something to do with company politics, a comedy interlude for the spectators or a means of making the steam-powered entrants look good? Possibly the latter, since Brandreth was a good friend of George Stephenson. But even this bizarre vehicle was later to find a home for a time with the South Carolina Railroad.

One of the key tests for the locomotives would be to pull or push loaded trucks up and down the test track until they had completed the equivalent of a return trip between Liverpool and Manchester. Judges carefully

Cyclopede, the token horse-powered entrant for the Rainhill trials. Original Illustration thought to be from *Mechanics Encyclopedia,* 1839.

recorded the time taken for servicing, any repairs needed and the fuel and water used. Only *Rocket* was able to complete this test unscathed, within the criteria set for the trial. But bad losers among the other candidates complained that *Rocket* had only been called upon to operate on the flat. So, on the morning of the seventh day of the trial, *Rocket*, with a carriage containing up to forty passengers, was taken to Sutton Incline - a 1:96 gradient just beyond the test track. Stephenson had always thought it to be impossible for locomotives and had intended to serve it by a stationary engine. But *Rocket* climbed it 'with ease' at 20mph (32km/h). On the flat, it had shown itself capable of 29mph (46km/h), pulling a 13-ton load. This must have been mind-boggling to an audience who previously had seen nothing faster than a galloping horse. The *Rocket's* average speed for the trial itself was 12mph (19km/h). Only 10mph (16km/h) was required to meet the trial criteria.

The outcome of the trial was in little doubt. *Rocket* was the only entrant to meet all of the judges' requirements and won the £500 prize. The others suffered from combinations of breakdowns, substandard performance or non-compliance with the trial rules. The reporters from the *Mechanics Magazine,* who were covering the event, were quite intoxi-

cated by the experience of speed, as they were whisked along at an un
precedented 30mph or thereabouts.

> We can say for ourselves that we never enjoyed anything in the way of
> travelling more. We flew along at the rate of a mile and a half in three min-
> utes; and although the velocity was such, that we could scarcely distinguish
> objects as we passed by them, the motion was so stable and equable, that we
> could manage not only to read, but to write.
>
> Quoted in Burton, 1980

But the correspondent of the *Mechanics Magazine* also forecast – utterly
wrongly – that *Novelty* was the shape of railway locomotives to come. In
fact, *Novelty*'s tiny boiler and bellows-assisted fire were already obsolete
and *Rocket* was to be the prototype for locomotives for the next 150 years.

But not everyone was intoxicated by the new sensation of speed.
The politician Thomas Creevy recorded his experience of travelling at
just 20mph:

> The quickest motion is to me frightful; it really is flying and it is impossible
> to divest yourself from the notion of instant death to all upon the least acci-
> dent happening. It gave me a headache which has not left me yet.
>
> Quoted in Faith

As for the Duke of Wellington, after the traumas of the opening day of the
Liverpool and Manchester Railway (what with Huskisson's death and the
Duke proving to be by no means the Manchester crowds' favourite politician)
it took thirteen years before he could be tempted back into a railway train.

The Stephensons were much happier. Not only did they win the Rainhill
prize, they also picked up an order for six more Rocket-type locomotives,
which they delivered in the summer of 1830. A seventh, *Northumbrian*, was
delivered just in time for the official opening of the railway, in September 1830.
The directors also bought *Sans Pareil* and *Novelty* – a further consolation
prize for their manufacturers. In a final twist, just three months after the
opening of the railway, Robert Stephenson announced a radically new
design of locomotive – named *Planet* – that rendered the design of all the
railway companies' newly bought locomotives obsolete.

Planet was Robert Stephenson's first big redesign after *Rocket*. It made every other locomotive seem out of date. This replica lives at the Manchester Museum of Science and Industry.

Each of the locomotives delivered by the Stephensons between Rainhill and the opening of the Liverpool and Manchester Railway had improvements on *Rocket*'s specification. It became clear that *Rocket* was not so much the finished article as a prototype. These changes were most marked in *Northumbrian*. This had the boiler and firebox made as a single unit, a separate smokebox (the first locomotive to do so) and a boiler with no fewer than 132 small-diameter tubes, giving three times the heating area of *Rocket*. For all the innovations introduced in *Rocket*, it had been made obsolete by 1833 by the developments of the *Planet* and *Patentee* designs.

News of the trial went round the world. This extract from the *Scotsman* newspaper sums up the importance attached to Rainhill:

> The experiments at Liverpool have established principles which will give a greater impulse to civilisation than it has ever received from any single cause since the press first opened the gates of knowledge to the human species at large.

The superiority of the steam railway locomotive over every other form of land-based transport had at last been demonstrated beyond any doubt, and the way was open for the transformation that it would bring to Victorian England. In fact, it was already happening in 1830. Several lines were already being planned around the central axis of the Liverpool and Manchester railway. One of these, the Warrington and Newton, planned to link Warrington to the Liverpool and Manchester, but also had later plans (for which they sought Robert Stephenson's help) to extend it to Sandbach and thence to Birmingham. This bought protests from the board of the Liverpool and Manchester, who had their own plans for extending their network to Birmingham. A route had been surveyed as long ago as 1825 and George Stephenson had been approached about overseeing this project just four days before the opening of the Liverpool and Manchester. The Stephensons were in a difficult situation. Clearly it was not for them to try and control an unregulated system, but were there legal or ethical problems for either of them acting as surveyors and advisors

Billy, a George Stephenson locomotive used in the building of the Liverpool and Manchester Railway, photographed in about 1862. It was in service from 1826 to about 1880, but *Billy* was obsolete before the Liverpool and Manchester Railway was even completed.

to two rival railway companies? Apparently not, for on this occasion they felt able to do just that.

The opening of the Liverpool and Manchester went ahead with eight Stephenson locomotives carrying 772 guests in the inaugural trains. The day was marred by the fatal injury to politician William Huskisson, who was rushed to Eccles and his eventual deathbed by train. In the course of this Stephenson set a new railway speed record of 36mph (He rounded it up to 40mph). Stephenson reflected on this with grim satisfaction later:

> Ten years ago my own counsel thought me fit for Bedlam for asserting that steam could propel locomotives at the rate of 10 miles an hour.

But Rainhill would not be the last locomotive competition. Eighteen months later the American Baltimore and Ohio Railway held one. Its weight limit was even stricter than Rainhill (3½ tons) but the test

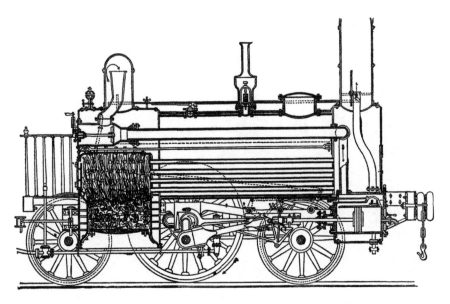

A cutaway picture of Stephenson's Standard Passenger engine of 1836, showing its working principles.

criteria were more realistic (thirty days' general service) and the prize money more generous ($4,000 first prize and $3,500 for the runner-up). The prize-winner was a watchmaker – Phineas Davis – and his engine *York* formed an initial class of locomotives for the railway that were not finally withdrawn until 1893.

The opening of the Liverpool and Manchester Railway, 1830.

5

Some Early Railways

In this chapter we look at some of the railways that pre-dated the Liverpool and Manchester Railway in 1830. These are just a sample of the many railways and wagonways that were built in the late eighteenth and early nineteenth centuries. Many of them had a lot in common – carrying coal or minerals from point of extraction to navigable waterway – but they also included some notable firsts: the first railway tunnel (outside of an actual mine) on the Butterley Gangroad (1793); the first example of containerisation on a railway at the Little Eaton Gangway (1795, the idea was originally dreamed up in 1766 by James Brindley); and even the first railway ferry (introduced by Ralph Allen in 1731 to ferry truckloads of stone from his quarry in Bath across the River Avon).

As we saw, in 1758 the **Middleton Collieries** of Leeds faced competition from a rival pit, which had the advantage of access to Leeds by river for the delivery of its coal. The then owner of Middleton, Charles Brandling, and his agent, Richard Humble, both came from Tyneside, where by this time wagonways were commonplace. Their natural response was therefore to build a wagonway, linking their pit to the river at Thwaite Gate, where it could be transhipped into barges for the final part of its journey.

Up to this time, colliery wagonways had generally been built across land in the control of the pit owner, or with the full support of the landowner, who probably leased the coal-bearing land to the person promoting the wagonway. Legally enforceable authority was therefore not needed to build the railway across anyone's land. But whilst Brandling's neighbours were generally supportive of his proposal, he must have been aware that this could change with a change in land ownership. Brandling therefore became the first person to obtain Parliamentary consent for the building of a railway.

31 Geo.2, c.xxii 9 June 1758 was 'An Act for establishing Agreement made between Charles Brandling, Esquire, and other persons, proprietors of lands, for laying down a wagon-way in order for the better supplying the Town and Neighbourhood of Leeds in the County of York, with coals'. It enabled Leeds to become a market-leading location for industries requiring copious amounts of coal, either for their manufacturing processes or to power their mill or factory machinery.

The wagonway was, with some qualifications discussed earlier, a success. It started as a wooden railway with horse-drawn wagons, but by 1799 the company had started to replace its wooden tracks with iron-edge rails built to a gauge of 4ft 1in (124.5cm). In 1812 it became the world's first commercial railway to make use of steam locomotives. But the colliery's then manager, John Blenkinsop, did not believe that a locomotive could be made light enough not to break the cast-iron rails, but still heavy enough to give the adhesion needed to pull a load of wagons. So Blenkinsop specified a rack-and-pinion system. Naturally, the world's first working steam railway also employed the world's first professional train driver – a former pit surface worker named James Hewitt, trained by the locomotive manufacturer.

It was a risky occupation. As we saw, in February 1818 one of the drivers made some unofficial adjustments to the safety valve, causing the boiler to explode and terminally hurling the driver a reported 100 yards into an adjoining field. Equally fatal was another explosion in February 1834, this time put down to inadequate maintenance, and taking the life of James Hewitt himself. The following year most of the pit reverted to horse traction, apart from a short section near the main pit served by a stationary steam engine. Steam was not reintroduced until 1866, and in 1881 the railway was converted to the standard (4ft 8½in) gauge, allowing it to be connected to the Midland Railway. It closed as part of the national rail network in July 1967, but was the following year bought by the Middleton Railway Trust, which now operates it as a preserved steam railway.

But was this the first railway? It depends on how you define it.

The **Lake Lock Rail Road** near Wakefield, Yorkshire, lays claim to being the world's first public railway, though others dispute that claim.

It was also claimed to be the world's first above-ground railway, being a 3-mile (4.8km) narrow-gauge railway (3ft 4¾in (103.5cm) gauge) running from Lake Rock on the Aire and Calder Navigation to Outwood. Its main purpose was the transhipment of coal and other raw materials, such as minerals. It was created under a Trust Deed, as a means of getting round the provisions of the South Sea Bubble Act of 1720, which was not repealed until 1825 (see Chapter 10). A deed is a legal document that creates a trust, giving a person or organisation the right to manage someone else's money or property. The deed sets out what the trustees are entitled to do with that property.

The Rail Road Company was formed in 1796 and opened to traffic in 1798, five years before the Surrey Iron Railway. Other railways (notably the Middleton) were older, but this one was built from the start for many independent operators to use, on payment of a toll – hence 'public'. The line had branches to collieries and a stone quarry, and the route was extended under a separate Act of Parliament in 1810. At its peak in about 1807, it was carrying 110,000 tons a year. But this went into a steady decline and the line was closed in 1836 when the main colliery owners built an alternative railway.

The **Carmarthenshire Railway** was authorised under an Act of Parliament on 3 June 1802. It lays claim to a number of firsts. It was the first railway to be approved by Act of Parliament in Wales. It became the first railway to own its own dock, when the company acquired the one at Llanelly and the tramroad to it, built by Alexander Raby in 1799. When its first section – from Cwmddyche ironworks to the harbour – opened in May 1803 it claimed to be the first stretch of public railway in use in Britain (although the Lake Lock Railway would dispute that). It was a 4ft-gauge (1,219mm), 11.8-mile-long (18.5km) horse-worked plateway, which closed in or before 1844, though parts of its route were later used for a steam railway.

The **Sirhowy Tramway** was a 4ft-gauge (121.9cm) plateway built to carry products from ironworks at Tredegar to Newport in south Wales. Part of the journey was made on a tramroad operated by the Monmouthshire Canal Company. It started life as a horse-drawn railway but became an early user of locomotive power. It was probably opened in 1805 (views differ) and was claimed to be the third public railway to be approved by Act of Parliament. By 1810 it had a custom-built passenger coach. It was designed to be single track with passing loops (or, as they called them, 'all convenient turnouts'). This was an advance on the local tramway that it replaced, which was purely single track. With the old tramway, empty wagons going up the hill would be manhandled off the line to make way for loaded wagons coming down the hill. It cost about £74,000 (or £3,000 per mile) to build, most of which was spent on a thirty-two-arch viaduct, known as 'the Long Bridge', across the Ebbw River and its flood-plain, and some very deep and expensive cuttings.

The tramway was profitable for many years, until all the other tramways in the valley were converted into standard-gauge railways. The Sirhowy got Parliamentary permission to follow suit in May 1860. A new route was built, passing through Blackwood and Argoed. Hitherto tramways had run through the main streets, having been built before those settlements had grown up. A number of the larger railway companies competed to take over the Sirhowy, and it finally became part of the LNWR in 1876. Falling passenger numbers due to bus competition led to the closure of passenger services in 1960, and the last few goods services ended in 1970.

The **Surrey Iron Railway** was built to overcome the transport deficiencies of the region. Mid-eighteenth-century Croydon was the principal town in east Surrey and an important market centre, where agricultural produce from a wide area was gathered for transhipment to London. However, the main Brighton road serving the area was 'so very ruinous and almost impassable for the space of five months in the year that it is dangerous for all persons, horses and other cattle to pass' (this from the Act of Incorporation of the Surrey and Sussex Turnpike Trust in 1718). The establishment of the Trust did not make things much better and by the late eighteenth century consideration was being given to building a canal.

Various schemes were put forward and the engineer John Rennie was engaged to draw up a detailed and costed route. This was taken to Parliament in February 1801, where a number of changes were made to it during its progress into law. These included clauses to protect the interests of mill owners on the River Wandle and rerouting the proposed canal to join the Grand Surrey Canal north of New Cross. The Croydon Canal Act received Royal Assent in June 1801, and the completed canal was fully opened to traffic in October 1809.

The fast-flowing waters of the River Wandle made it ideal for powering mills, and it also attracted a host of other industries. In 1805 there were an estimated fifty manufacturers along its 10-mile length, employing upwards of 1,700 people. These companies were still concerned about the difficulty of getting their products to market in London. Their thoughts turned initially to further canal building and a leading canal engineer of the day, William Jessop, was engaged to investigate the possibility. He concluded that the water for any canal would have to be drawn from the Wandle and that the opposition to this from the businesses along the river would be unavoidable and insuperable. There was, however, a possible alternative – the adoption of an iron railway. According to Jessop, these had been in use for many years in the north of England, chiefly at coal mines and 'it is but lately that they have been brought into the degree of perfection, which now recommends them as substitutes for canals'.

What Jessop was proposing was quite novel: a self-contained public railway, not for use as part of a mine or quarry or as part of a canal system. Jessop had experience of building such iron railways – the Forest Line of the Leicester Navigation (opened in 1794) was engineered by him, and even used edge rails. The subscribers to the Surrey scheme voted in 1800 to build an iron railway and Jessop was appointed its engineer. It was approved in May 1801, under the memorable title of 'An Act for making and maintaining a Railway from the Town of Wandsworth to the Town of Croydon, with a Collateral Branch onto the Parish of Carshalton, and a Navigable Communication between the River Thames and the said Railway at Wandsworth, all in the County of Surrey (41 Geo. III cap.33)'. It was the first act to permit a genuinely public railway, independent of a canal, and to incorporate a railway company.

Benjamin Outram and Company tendered unsuccessfully for the construction works and the name(s) of the successful constructor(s) are not known. Work initially proceeded rapidly, but was then held up by the delayed delivery of rails. However, part of the railway was opened by July 1802 and the whole line was officially opened in July 1803. A press report in the *Hampshire Telegraph* said the committee went up in wagons drawn 'by one horse; and to show how motion is facilitated by this ingenious yet simple contrivance, a gentleman, with two companions, drove up the railway, in a machine of his own invention, without horses, at the rate of fifteen miles an hour'. (This was thought to have been some kind of handcart with hand or foot controls.)

The Surrey Iron Railway was an early example of a double-track railway with some additional refinements, as this early account of its operation shows:

> Thus far it is nearly complete, with a double railway; that is, the one being used for the passage outwards, and the other for the return, without obstructing each other, as would be the case if there was only one road; they have nevertheless, at certain distances, a method for letting the waggons pass from one road to the other by a short diagonal railway, and by throwing or forcing aside a bar of iron moving on a pivot, which enables them to move in and out with the greatest facility.
>
> James Malcolm, *A Compendium of Modern Husbandry*, Vol. 1 1805

It was a public toll railway, on which independent hauliers used their own horses and wagons. The company did not operate its own trains. The railway had a gauge of 4ft 2in (127cm) and a spacing of about 5ft between the centres of the stone blocks on which the rails were mounted. The coming of faster, more powerful and heavier steam locomotives spelt the end for horse-drawn railways. William James, a shareholder, tried to persuade George Stephenson to provide a steam locomotive but Stephenson declined, on the grounds that the cast-iron plateway would not bear the weight of a locomotive. Attempts were made to sell the railway to the London and Brighton Railway, so that they could use part of its route to extend their own trackbed. But the sale was not completed and in August 1846, with Parliament's blessing, the railway was closed.

Oystermouth Railway (1806), the world's first passenger railway service, was built under an 1804 Act of Parliament to carry limestone from a quarry at Mumbles, and coal from the Clyne Valley, to Swansea. From there it would be transhipped to the Swansea Canal and other markets. It was called the Oystermouth Railway after a tiny fishing village along the route. One of the leading lights in its promotion was the copper and coal magnate John (later Sir John) Morris, Bart. The enabling act permits haulage by 'men, horses or otherwise' – a fairly common form of wording on Railway Acts of this era, though the founders can surely have had no other option but horse power in mind. But, oddly enough, a short-lived attempt was actually made to run the railway by sail power.

An old and important image of a horse-drawn train on the Oystermouth Railway, *c.*1855.

Passengers came into the equation in 1807, when Benjamin French, one of the company's shareholders, paid the company £20 a year (more than £1,200 in modern terms) for the right to carry passengers. From 25 March passengers could pay 5*d* (more than £3 in today's money) for the privilege of travelling the route in a converted goods wagon. The service was a great success, leading Mr French to up his offer to £25 for the following year's licence. Quite how comfortable a ride you got for your money seems to be open to question. A traveller using the route in 1813 said the sixteen-seater carriage made the noise of 'twenty sledge hammers in full play' and that he emerged from the ordeal ' in a state of dizziness and confusion of the sense that it is well if he recovers from it in a week' (Ayton and Daniell, 1814).

The building of a turnpike road in parallel to the railway in the mid 1820s took away most of its passenger traffic, and a cheaper bus service along the turnpike was the final straw. The passenger service closed in 1826 or 1827.

In the early days the railway operated like the canals and turnpikes of the day. The Parliamentary Act setting up the railway laid down a schedule of tolls and charges, and anyone with a suitable wagon and the toll money could use it. The original railway was a plateway of approximately 4ft (121.9cm) gauge, though it was rebuilt, with edge rails and a standard 4ft 8½in (143.5cm) gauge, in about 1855. The new railway reintroduced a horse-drawn passenger service. Steam power began to replace horses, using Henry Hughes' patent tramway locomotives, though this was not completed until 1896, due to a dispute with the Swansea Tramways and Improvements Company.

Traffic on the railway began to decline as the pits that different branches served were closed. The Clyne valley branch fell into disuse after the Rhydydefaid pit was shut down. But at the same time a new concern – the Mumbles Railway and Pier Company – was set up to extend the railway beyond Oystermouth to a new pier close to Mumbles Head. This was fully opened, including the pier, in 1898.

A miscellaneous assortment of steam locomotives ran the services between 1877 and 1929, when the line was electrified, using overhead transmission. The vehicles used – Brush Electrical double-bogie two-deck tramcars – each carried 106 passengers, making them the largest cars built for service in Britain. In 1958 the railway was bought out by the South Wales Transport Company (the main local bus operator), and the following year it went to Parliament with an Abandonment Bill, which became the South Wales Transport Act 1959. The last train along the line (a special for local dignitaries) ran on 5 January 1960.

At the time of its closure the Oystermouth was claimed to be the world's longest-serving railway, though others, such as the Middleton, which carried only goods, pre-dated it. But it is the oldest passenger railway.

The **Newcastle and Carlisle Railway Company (1835)** very nearly had a more prominent (that is, early) place among the list of pioneering railways. Eighteenth-century Carlisle was a major commercial centre by the standards of the day, but suffered from the town's river, the Eden, being unsuitable for navigation. William Chapman, an engineer otherwise best known for inventing the bogie and for articulated rail vehicles, surveyed and published a route for a canal in 1795, bypassing the unnavigable parts of the river. It got as far as Parliament in 1797 but was opposed and withdrawn. A shorter canal, from Bowness to Carlisle, was approved and opened in 1823. Bowness was renamed Port Carlisle, but the canal was only large enough to carry small ships.

J. W. Carmichael, del.   II. Griffiths, sc.

Early Travelling on the Newcastle and Carlisle Railway.

Views on the Newcastle and Carlisle Railway. (J.W. Carmichael, 1836)

In 1805 William Thomas came up with an idea for a horse-operated plateway from Newcastle to Hexham. The idea came to nothing in the short term, but railways and steam power generally were very much in favour locally and in 1824 William Chapman's idea of a link between Newcastle and Carlisle re-emerged, but this time as a railway, rather than a canal. For the most part the railway followed the proposed canal route, substituting flights of locks by rope-hauled inclined planes. But the biggest difference was in the cost. Chapman priced the railway at £252,000, against £888,000 for the canal. A later, independent review of the costs by Josias Jessop increased the railway costs to £292,000 and then to £300,000. Jessop also made some changes to the route. A railway company was formed in 1825 and fund-raising began.

Submission to Parliament in 1826 was delayed by opposition from the landed gentry and from George Stephenson (who was surveying a rival route), as well as a weak money market. At this stage, it was intended to run the railway on an open house toll-road system. To address the opposition from the landed gentry, the company volunteered to limit the railway to horse traction and to ban the erection of stationary steam engines near to their stately homes.

Construction proceeded, but difficulty getting shareholders to pay up the stage payments on their shares added to the company's pre-existing cashflow problems. These were exacerbated when the company had to raise extra funds to cover cost overruns. However, the first section of line, from Hexham to Blaydon, opened in 1835. An attempt to introduce steam haulage (which was then still unlawful under the earlier agreement) attracted a further legal challenge. It took another Act of Parliament and a huge groundswell of pro-railway public support to get the restriction removed, later that year. Further extensions to the line opened in the next few years and in June 1838 the first trains ran between Newcastle and Carlisle. Torrential rain and a train collision marred the opening day.

The line has one further claim to fame. Early railways wrote tickets by hand, gathering copious information such as name, address, age, occupation and reason for travelling. These were all useful (for example, in locating next of kin in the event of an accident). It was Thomas Edmondson, a stationmaster for the Newcastle and Carlisle Railway, who came up with the system for using preprinted tickets that was used throughout British Railways until 1984. Edmondson received a royalty on every mile of railway track on which they were used, and died a wealthy man.

The **Stockton and Darlington Railway (1825)** was not the first passenger-carrying railway, nor the first public freight railway, and *Locomotion No. 1* was not the first steam locomotive. But it was the first public railway to carry passengers and freight using steam locomotion. Even then, passenger coaches had to rely on horse power until 1833, when steam haulage was introduced. Even the name Stockton and Darlington was something of a misnomer. There was more of the railway to the west of Darlington, going out to the coalfields, than there was between the towns of Stockton and Darlington themselves. Darlington only became the railway's headquarters because the Pease family (who did so much to promote and fund the railway) had their family businesses based there.

Opening day of the Stockton and Darlington Railway, 1825.

The fundamental reason for the railway was to enable the coalfields of west Durham to compete with their neighbours to the east. The east Durham coal measures were deeper underground but closer to navigable water for transhipment to London and other markets. West Durham coal being taken to coastal ports faced long journeys along poor roads or a River Tees that was difficult to navigate (due to tidal flows and shifting sand bars). This was the case even after the 'New cut' of 1810, in which 2¼ miles of the meandering river had been replaced by 200 yards of canal. Various combinations of canals and tramways were considered, until November 1818, when the Welsh engineer George Overton's survey options led the promoters to come down in favour of a rail-based solution.

Edward Pease's 19-year-old son, Joseph, drew up a prospectus, estimated costings and receipts were produced and, within a week, £25,000 of the estimated £113,000 cost had been subscribed. A railway bill was submitted to Parliament.

The death of King George III (leading to a dissolution of Parliament and a general election) delayed consideration of the Bill until the 1820–21 session of Parliament, but it received Royal Assent on 19 April 1821. This authorised 'making and maintaining a Railway or Tramroad from the River Tees at Stockton, to Witton Park Colliery with several Branches therefrom, all in the county of Durham'. The act ran to sixty-seven pages, specifying the wording and even the size of the lettering on the sides of the wagons, the construction of any building needed for the railway, and the tolls and charges it could make. It also gave any landowner within 5 miles of the railway the right to build their own branch line connecting with the main route – more monopoly phobia on the part of the legislators.

Overton was then replaced by George Stephenson, who was asked to resurvey the route. This he did by the end of 1821. He submitted his report and four days later was appointed engineer at £660 per annum. A second Act of Parliament was needed to approve Stephenson's proposed route changes, and also to permit the use of 'loco-motive or moveable Engines' – one topic on which the first act had been notably (if unsurprisingly) silent. Orders were placed with Stephenson and Company, initially for two locomotives at £500 each. By September 1825 the railway was in a sufficient state of readiness to be officially opened. This took place on 27 September, after a frantic few days to get everything, in particular the solitary locomotive, running. At one stage, the company found that it did not have any means of lighting the locomotives' fire, and had to improvise by focusing the sun's rays through a magnifying glass onto a pile of wood shavings.

Stephenson's many other commitments meant that the responsibility for the day-to-day running of the railway fell upon the company's newly appointed locomotive foreman, Timothy Hackworth. Most of the initial services had to be horse-drawn, the company having only one unreliable locomotive. However, Stephensons delivered a second – called *Hope* – in November 1825 and two further locomotives – later named *Black Diamond* and *Diligence* – in spring 1826.

Initial arrangements for passengers were primitive in the extreme. After a few months of running their passenger carriage *Experiment* (essentially a stagecoach with couplings for horses at either end), they decided to put the passenger service out to contractors. *Experiment* was let to one Richard Pickersgill for £200 a year. There were no stations; at Darlington they started from a point described as 'near the Great North Road' and the Stockton terminus was 'the riverbank near Stockton Wharf'. Intermediate stops were made by would-be passengers flagging down the coach, usually outside one of the trackside inns. The passengers' discomfort would be completed by the less affluent of them having to occupy one of the cheaper outside seats of the coach, whatever the weather. Even the locomotive men and the coach drivers had no weather protection. Nonetheless, so popular were they that more services had to be added. By September 1833 they had decided to bring the passenger service back in-house and to use steam haulage. The coach proprietors had to be bought out, at a cost of £316 17s 8d (£316.87).

Many other aspects of the operation would strike the modern reader as primitive. It was another of those operated on the turnpike system, whereby anyone with the toll money and a wagon of the right gauge had a right to use it. There were no signals until 1840, when a solitary one was introduced; no reliable timetables for services existed and the locomotives had no brakes, until Timothy Hackworth's improved locomotives began to be introduced. Drivers needing to stop quickly had to rely on the brutal expedient of throwing the locomotive into reverse. As for the points, they had to be held in place with a stick while the train passed over them, risking derailment and/or serious injury to the railwayman.

The track was single line with four passing places per mile, and there were countless cases of violent disputes, as trains came head to head, about who had priority. The rules were supposed to be that steam had priority over horse power but passengers had priority over coal. Also, the vehicle reaching the designated midway point between passing places first had right of way. If traffic going in the opposite direction were not complicated enough, horse-drawn coaches held up steam trains going in the same direction and malfunctioning steam locomotives held up horse-drawn coaches. There were initially no fixed standards for buffers or couplings, leading to unnecessary damage to rolling stock and difficulty in assembling trains. All this inefficiency added to delays and queueing – sometimes on the main line. The average time taken for a wagon to cover the 26¾ miles between Bishop Auckland and Stockton rose to four and a half days. In 1833 Timothy Hackworth was promoted from locomotive foreman to general manager to try and sort these and other problems out.

One further development for the region's economy was Joseph Pease's purchase in 1829 of 527 acres of farmland downstream of Stockton. This was to become the great iron-manufacturing city of Middlesbrough, which was effectively created by the Stockton and Darlington Railway.

The **Canterbury and Whitstable Railway**, known to the locals as the 'Crab and Winkle line', opened (as its name suggests) between the centre of Canterbury and Whitstable harbour in 1830, just four months before the Liverpool and Manchester. It was from the outset a public railway and was intended for the carriage of both passengers and freight. The construction of the line was approved by Parliament in June 1825, and three further acts, of 1827, 1828 and 1835, allowed for the issue of a further £80,000 of stock, as construction costs escalated. But, unlike the Liverpool and Manchester, much of its journey was to be cable-hauled by stationary engines, with locomotive steam used only on a level stretch of the 6-mile route.

Up until then, Canterbury had been mainly reliant upon the River Stour for the delivery of goods. Although it is only 17 miles (27km) as the crow flies to Ramsgate, near to where the river reaches the Kentish coast, the meandering river route covers about 70 miles (110km). To make matters worse, the river was prone to silting up and the cost of dredging 70 miles of river was prohibitive. There were turnpikes link-ing the two settlements, but it would require four or five carts to carry the load of a single barge, making that unviable as a main supply line to Canterbury.

At 7 miles (11km) due north from Canterbury, Whitstable was a shorter route to the sea. The problem was that the land between the two rose sharply to a height of 200ft (61m), beyond the capability of the loco-motives of the day – hence the reliance on stationary steam engines. A longer, locomotive-friendly alternative route, through Sturry, Herne and Swalecliffe, would have been prohibitively expensive in terms of land acquisition and construction costs.

Whitstable was at that time a small village and port. Its main trade was in iron pyrites from the Isle of Sheppey. The idea for the railway came from the pioneering railway promoter William James, who drew up plans for improving the harbour and linking it to the railway. The route James surveyed must have looked daunting to the railwaymen of the day:

- From central Canterbury the line would climb 1 mile 70 chains (3.02km) at a rate of 1:46 to Tyler Hill, where there were two 25hp winding engines and a 828-yd (757m) tunnel – the world's first tunnel on a steam-hauled passenger line;
- For the next 1 mile 10 chains (1.81km) the gradient eased to a more manageable 1:750. At the summit of the line at Clowes Wood there was a 15hp winding engine;
- The line descended for a mile (1.61km) at 1:31, to a level stretch of 1 mile 20 chains (2.01km);
- It then descended again at 1:53 for 40 chains (0.8km) to a final level section of 20 chains (0.4km) into Whitstable.

All this within a journey of 6 miles (9.66km).

George Stephenson was appointed chief engineer of the line, at a time when he was more than fully occupied with other matters, such as the Stockton and Darlington and Liverpool and Manchester lines. John Dixon was his deputy (and did most of the work). Stephenson (or Dixon?) specified a horse-drawn service along the level sections of the route but the promoters overruled him as far as the shallowest incline was concerned, insisting on ordering a steam locomotive from Robert Stephenson and Co.

What they got was *Invicta*, the twentieth locomotive from that manufacturer, built immediately after *Rocket*, with which it shares many design features. The locomotive is discussed in more detail elsewhere in the book. Suffice it to say here that its name (Latin for *undefeated*, the motto on the county flag of Kent) was a gross misnomer. It was defeated by the mildest of inclines on the railway and, following an ill-considered rebuild that actually made its performance worse, it was withdrawn in 1839, replaced by an additional stationary engine.

The major civil engineering challenge on the railway was the Tyler Hill tunnel. The two teams of tunnellers made contact with each other in

May 1827, almost two years after Royal Assent, but on 15 June a large section of the roof caved in. The promoters of the railway had seriously under-estimated the cost of building it and repeatedly had to delay completion while they went back to Parliament for authority to raise additional funds. Not until 3 May 1830 was it in a fit state to receive locomotives. One feature of the tunnel was a rising gradient of 1:56 towards Whitstable, and this resulted in it becoming embroiled in a dispute between Isambard Kingdom Brunel (who had nothing to do with the actual building of this railway) and his would-be nemesis, Dionysius Lardner.

Lardner was professor of natural philosophy and astronomy at University College London, and a great populariser of science. Unfortunately, the science he popularised was often wrong and the railway tunnel argument was just one of the public fallings-out Lardner had with Brunel in which he was left looking foolish. As part of his Great Western Railway, Brunel planned the Box Tunnel, which had a slope of 1:100 (about half that of the Tyler Hill Tunnel). Lardner claimed that if a train's brakes were to fail in the tunnel, it would accelerate to over 120mph, break up and kill all the passengers (those who had not already been suffocated by the unnatural speeds at which they were travelling). Brunel was able to point out Lardner's schoolboy error, of omitting air resistance and friction from his calculations. As a practical demonstration, he sent a carriage freewheeling through the Tyler Hill Tunnel, proving that his own calculations were correct. One thing the designers of the tunnel got wrong was its loading gauge. Although the tracks were laid to the standard gauge, they only allowed for a 12ft (3.7m) headroom, which was not high enough for modern locomotives; specially cut-down locos had to be made to operate the line.

The railway finally opened on 3 May 1830, a single-track line with two passing places along its 6-mile route. At this time, the Stephensons' preferred method of mounting the rails was on stone blocks. But there was no suitable stone within easy reach of the railway, making that option too expensive. They had to resort instead to wooden sleepers.

The line was never a great success, and was near to bankruptcy when it was taken over by the South East Railway in the 1840s. It was further set back when the London, Chatham and Dover Railway opened in 1860, offering better services between Whitstable and London. Passenger services along it ceased at the beginning of 1931 and the line was closed entirely in December 1952 (apart from a short reprieve, following flooding elsewhere in the network in 1953). Most traces of its existence have now gone. The University of Kent now stands on the hilltop above the Tyler Hill Tunnel, part of which has been filled in to prevent subsidence.

6

Some Lessons from Canal Mania

In other chapters, we have seen how developments in fields such as mining have contributed, directly or indirectly, to the development of steam railways. Here we will look at the relationship between the canals and the first railways.

As we will see, within little more than a lifetime Britain experienced three major transport revolutions. One of them gave us the era of the canals, another the high points of the turnpike road revolution and the third the birth of the railway network. The similarities between the birth pangs of the canals and those of the railways in particular are quite striking and the knowledge accumulated from canal-building made its own contribution to the development of the railway network – or at least it could have done, if the lessons from it had always been learned. We will look briefly at just a few of these, but first a few words on the strengths and weaknesses of canals as a rival mode of transport to rail.

The nation's waterways, including the waters surrounding our coasts, have long been some of our most important corridors of trade. The benefits were evident; a packhorse with a load strapped to its back could carry no more than ⅛ tonne (a tonne being a metric ton, or 1,000 kilos). A horse and cart on a well-made road might pull 2 tonnes; but on a waterway a horse-drawn boat might tow a load of up to 40 tonnes (or possibly even 50 on the still waters of a canal).

But a system based on natural waterways had its drawbacks. There were not always navigable waterways wherever you wanted to go to or from; even if there were, they were unlikely to go directly to your destination, and the meanders of a river could add considerably to the length of the navigation. Rivers or canals might be made difficult or impossible by rapids or shallows, by droughts in summer, ice in winter, tides on coastal waters or currents on natural or 'improved' waterways all year round. Waiting to pass through locks would build in delays to the journey (albeit that they helped manage the water supply and thus guaranteed a more certain passage along the waterway). There may be competing users of the waterway, whose needs conflicted with those of barges and other river traffic. These included fishermen and their nets and, in particular, the 10,000 mills listed in the Domesday Book in England, who would block the rivers with their dams, only releasing the water to suit their business needs (or if suitably bribed by the bargee).

From as early as Roman times, efforts were made to improve the natural waterways for navigation. Impassable sections were made passable; new channels were dug to shorten meandering rivers; locks and weirs were installed to manage the flow of the river better and to enable laden vessels to pass over shallow stretches. Flooding was managed and attempts were made (with varying degrees of success) to resolve the conflicts between different river users. But the real drive for improvement started in the sixteenth century, as the population and trade (and with it the volume of business travel) increased and the shocking state of the nation's transport infrastructure was thrown into sharp relief.

A number of existing canals or canalised rivers were improved, by shortcutting meanders and bypassing unnecessary locks, or putting in aqueducts or inclined planes. Twenty-nine river navigation improvements were undertaken in the sixteenth and seventeenth centuries, all of them based on existing waterways. They brought most of England (with notable exceptions such as Birmingham and parts of Staffordshire) within 15 miles (24km) of a navigable waterway. They need not delay us for the purpose of this present book, except to say that their improvements became ever more sophisticated. They pointed the way towards a completely 'artificial' canal, one based more directly on where the traffic wanted to go, rather than whether there was an existing watercourse for the promoters to 'improve'.

What should not be forgotten is the extent to which the boom years of the canals also acted as a stimulus to railway building. Digging a length of canal could be a costly undertaking (typically three times that of a railway, or more if the topography it ran through were difficult). Many areas had a topography that was so steeply inclined that any canal would be, if not physically impossible, unfeasibly costly to build and slow to operate.

Slow to build, slow to operate; a canal might also be less attractive than a railway to some investors. Nicholas Wood in 1831 quoted the example of a tramway running from Brynmawr to the Brecon Canal. Although a mere ancillary to the canal, and built in a matter of months rather than years, the tramway company was able to pay a 5 per cent dividend, whereas the canal company's dividends never got above 0.5 per cent.

Rather than building a branch canal to join up with the main route, it might prove to be less expensive to provide a short horse-drawn railway to link the waterway to nearby businesses. This was what happened to the Glamorganshire Canal, where we saw an early example of the relationship between canals and railways. The tramway built would be known as Penydarren, and was the one on which in 1804 the world's first working railway journey took place (described earlier in the book).

As railways became more common and more sophisticated, competition from them was not always unwelcome to canal investors. For example, the Oakham Canal, between Melton Mowbray and Oakham in Rutland, was opened in 1802, but was never a financial success. Its potential markets were limited and its water supply unreliable – it was closed for nearly five months one dry summer. Its original investors paid £130 per share but received only £12 per share in dividends in the first forty years of its operation. So when the Midland Railway came along with proposals to build a line between Syston and Peterborough along part of its (drained) length the canal shareholders were enthusiastic. The construction of the railway, and the consequential closure and abandonment of the canal were approved by Parliament in 1846, and the sale of the canal completed in 1847. The railway from Melton Mowbray to Oakham opened in 1848, running along part of the original canal bed, and the long-suffering canal shareholders at least got a final distribution of £44.35 per share on their original investment.

A similar fate befell the Blaenavon Canal Navigation, approved as a waterway in 1792. Between 1850 and 1855 the Monmouthshire Canal

Navigation Company became the Monmouthshire Railway and Canal Company, and the canal became a 5-mile stretch of what became known as the Eastern Valleys Railway.

So what lessons might the promoters of, and investors in, the early railways have learned from an earlier generation of canal builders?

Funding

The Duke of Bridgewater self-funded the Bridgewater Canal and, despite being by no means a poor man, nearly bankrupted himself in the process. Those that followed him generally did so through a development company and shareholders. The Trent and Mersey raised £130,000 through the sale of £200 shares, and the Birmingham Canal Company in 1767 raised £70,000 in £140 shares, with no shareholder being allowed to hold more than ten. Canals serving local interests were especially popular investments for local businessmen. Some could be seriously over-subscribed:

> At a late meeting of subscribers to the Rochdale Canal £53,000 was immediately raised … and so unanimous are the gentlemen in the neighbourhood for carrying it into effect, that three times that sum can be forthcoming whenever it is necessary.
>
> *The Times*, 4 January 1791

Canal shares certainly came to be seen by speculators as a licence to print money. The Birmingham shares, mentioned above, priced at £140 in 1767, had gone up to £370 in 1782 and £1,170 by 1792. Originally, reference to there being investor interest could be taken as a mark of a sound proposal, but the investors were increasingly overtaken by speculators and gamblers, and sound investment tipped over into canal mania, the predecessor to the railway mania of the 1830s and 1840s. Nor did the interest in canals suddenly evaporate with the coming of the first railways. More miles of canal than railway were still being built in the 1830s.

Cliques of in-the-know would-be investors would meet in conditions of deepest secrecy to plan the launch of their canal scheme, laying down false trails to stop any outsider 'getting in on a good thing'. Would-be speculators, meanwhile, would be chasing round the countryside, following up every rumour of a possible shareholder meeting. It did not seem to matter much where the waterway was going to or from, provided it had the name 'canal' in its title. Speculators with no hope of affording to buy shares outright could make money simply by signing up to subscribe to a given share issue and immediately signing it over to a third party. In the peak year of 1793, thirty-six canal bills were submitted to Parliament, nineteen of which got Royal Assent. The nation looked like being awash with canals. As one Member of Parliament put it 'he wished his grandchildren might be born web-footed that they might be able to swim in water, for there would not be a bit of dry land in the island to walk upon'.

At its peak, the canal network would extend to some 4,000 miles but, as in the case of railway mania later, it all ended in tears. A trade recession and the outbreak of war knocked the bottom out of the canal market. Many of the schemes were in trouble, and so were many of the shareholders, left holding share certificates they could not afford, having meant to offload them onto someone even more gullible than themselves before having to pay for them, but failing to do so before the crash. One consequence of this was a general lowering of share prices, the entry level for share owner ship falling from, say, £200 to as low as £1. But these small investors scarcely made a dent in the financial needs of the canal; the vast majority came from big merchants and merchant banks. So the first lesson that might be learned from canal mania was one for the gambling public – the time when the impoverished speculator in shares starts to get interested in your area of business is very probably the time to get out.

Even after they had raised the estimated cost of the scheme, the canal company's financial problems were not necessarily over. Banks were not as secure in the eighteenth century as they are today, and the company's treasurer – effectively the canal's banker – had a huge amount of responsibility, which not every one of them discharged responsibly. Many problems could face a canal company working on a long-term project to a fixed budget. Unforeseen construction difficulties were one, but a more common one was fixed-price contracts at a time of inflation. Thomas Telford provided detailed figures for the Caledonian Canal, showing how dramatically wages and material costs had risen between 1803 and 1812 – by more than a half in many cases.

One option for canals was to call upon their existing investors to pay more; but many would refuse to do so, preferring in some cases to forfeit their original investment, rather than invest further. The Huddersfield Canal was one that staggered on from one financial crisis, and one short-term financial fix, to another, for years. This canal, originally proposed in the 1790s, was not finished until 1811. Other canals fared even worse, being only partly finished, or even abandoned. The problem was compounded by the fact that there were now more attractive and secure investments to be had, not least from the government. So the second lesson, this one for the railway promoters, was to budget for inflation and, if in doubt, be pessimistic.

One final and positive side-effect of the financing of canals is that it created a small group of men with expertise in handling the vast sums of money involved. During the canal mania years of 1788 to 1795 more than £6 million was subscribed for canals and a further £2 million borrowed. Some of this expertise would come in useful during the railway age – except where its lessons were ignored.

Parliamentary Procedures

The flood of canal bills received by Parliament in the early 1790s led to them introducing a special set of standing orders in 1792, designed to streamline the processing of all the applications. The standing orders included advertising the scheme in all the local papers affected by it, and in the *London Gazette*, and placing on deposit maps of the scheme, a list of property owners affected and the estimated costs. In the Parliamentary committees themselves, arguments were to be taken away from lay people and put in the hands of specialist lawyers, which allowed the debate to become more complex and technical. This all meant that the debate became ever more time-consuming; the Dudley Canal Bill spent twenty-three days being examined by the Lords. As we will see, these all seem remarkably similar to the preparatory work required of the railway bills years later.

One lesson railway promoters learned from the canals was that they needed to have at least one man full-time in Westminster, to coordinate all the people their cause relied upon, to pay lawyers' fees and witnesses' expenses and to grease palms where necessary. Burton recalls that the Duke of Bridgewater's canal accounts include suspiciously vague payments to someone going under the name of 'Mr Bill'. They might also have anticipated, and made something like the budgetary provision needed, for the cost of getting their schemes through the Parliamentary process, if that cost could even be guessed at.

Engineering

The engineering challenges canal engineers faced were remarkably similar to those that would confront early railway builders years later. They were both looking, ideally, for the shortest and flattest route between A and B, and having to cope with the hills and valleys, water courses, awkward landowners, poor ground conditions and built-up areas that got in the way of that ideal direct route. Both had to seek out flat routes, since neither canal barges nor early steam locomotives could cope easily with gradients; and they had to develop a similar range of civil engineering techniques to do so – tunnels, embankments, viaducts/aqueducts and cuttings.

The aqueduct posed problems for the canal engineer that the railway engineer might not have to deal with on such a regular basis, for example in terms of water pressure on the sides of the aqueduct. One further consideration for the canal builder was water supply. There must be sufficient supplies of water available at all times if the canal is not to run dry. Burton estimated that every boat passing through the Grand Junction Canal and its locks used up 112,000 gallons of water. That water has to come from a reliable and unsullied supply somewhere nearby and be stored somewhere equally convenient. This in itself could involve large-scale engineering – the Killington reservoir on the Lancaster Canal, for example, had a capacity of 700 million gallons – the equivalent of 17.5 million car tanks' full.

The skills of the canal engineer and the railway engineer were thus largely interchangeable, and a number of them – John Rennie, William Cubitt, William Jessop and Benjamin Outram, to name but four – made distinguished contributions to both branches of engineering. The finest achievements of the canal age rivalled anything the railways would go on to produce. To take just two examples, the eighteen-arched Pontcysyllte aqueduct on the Ellesmere Canal stretched 336 yards (307m) and is the nation's oldest and longest aqueduct, and the world's tallest. Completed in 1805, it is today a World Heritage site. As for tunnels, the canal promoters built twenty of more than half a mile in length. The longest, Standedge on the Huddersfield Narrow Canal, measured 3 miles 176 yards (5,029m). It was completed in 1811 at a cost of £160,000, the most costly tunnel of its day and one that was not surpassed in length by any railway tunnel until 1886. Canal tunnels could have unexpected security problems, from people wishing to harm either themselves or the infrastructure. The Glenfield tunnel on the Leicester and Swannington Canal was given security gates at one end and a manned tunnel security house at the other.

Labour Relations

Labour relations could be a challenge for the builders of both canals and railways. Much of the day-to-day grief of contract management would be borne by the resident engineer, who was a subordinate of the chief engineer. Labour relations with the navvies could be difficult, not least because they worked for the contractor, not the engineer. The Lancaster Canal in June 1796 had thirty-five different contractors working on it, and this was not an unusually high number. They managed workforces ranging in size from 150 to two, and part of the engineer's problem could be finding anyone to whom he could give orders. If the engineer despaired of ever finding the contractor's agent and issued orders direct to the workmen, he risked a whole new industrial dispute. Workmen tended not to want to be removed from the contractor's control and managed directly by the engineer, since they relied on the contractor to move them on from one canal job to the next.

The resident engineer thus became the lightning conductor for every kind of complaint and dispute – carters who failed to deliver essential materials on time, contractors who damaged local roads, paying off local residents for every kind of disturbance and complaint (real or imagined), or measuring the work done (given that contractors were paid by work done, rather than time spent, and the engineer's measurements of progress invariably came out lower than those of the contractor). In between all this, the resident engineer might even find time to tackle some actual engineering problems, such as quality control of the completed works.

By the turn of the nineteenth century, at a conservative estimate there were well over 50,000 labourers employed in canal work. Farmers petitioned Parliament to stop this drain on their sector, particularly at key times such as harvest. The navvies were widely demonised, and not always justly. Part of the problem lay with mistreatment on the part of the contractors who employed them or the local businesses that served (and sometimes tried to swindle) them. Another factor was the repressive policies of the governments of the period, which meant, among other things, that a fair number of the navvies were fugitives from what passed for justice (the anonymity of navvying being a good place to hide). Arguably the largest part of the problem stemmed from the nature of their job and the conditions of their employment. As Burton put it:

> Take thousands of poor, uneducated men, remove them from home and family, send them out into the wilds to sweat away at hard, dirty and dangerous work, and you cannot be too surprised if the end product is a gang of men who frequently find their release in outbursts of drunkenness and fighting.
>
> Burton, 2015

Whatever the causes, the coming of the navvies to an area, whether to dig a canal or build a railway, was generally received with great trepidation by that community, and could even lead to hostility to the very idea of the community being joined to the national transport network, whatever its longer-term benefits. A few contractors made attempts to get their navvies placed in lodging houses, as an attempt to provide them with at least a tenuous link with normal life, but as their numbers grew and grew even this modest effort foundered.

Perhaps the main lesson about labour relations and the navvies from the canal years is one clearly taken on board by the great railway entrepreneur turned Member of Parliament, Samuel Peto:

I know that if you pay him well, and show him you care for him, he is the most faithful and hardworking creature in existence ... give him legitimate occupation, and remuneration for his services, show him you appreciate those services, and you may be sure to put an end to all agitation. He will be your faithful servant.

Peto, addressing the opening of Parliament in 1851

A Canal Network

Two final lessons the early railways could learn from the canals were:

- The need to ensure a national standard gauge, so that the nation's network could really function as such, and
- to future-proof the network against growing demand for it.

The Bridgewater Canal, as originally constructed, was built to take boats of up to 14ft 6in beam and relatively unlimited length (there being no locks along its 41 miles). But this was not adopted as a national standard, which would have allowed boats of that size to have free passage around the nation's waterways. Just over a quarter of Britain's waterways were built to a much smaller standard, of 7ft wide: (a) because investors were nervous about the business potential of the early canals, and thought that a smaller canal would be cheaper and thus less risky financially, and (b) possibly because of the early precedent for a 7ft width set by James Brindley from 1770, when building the Harecastle Tunnel on the Trent and Mersey Canal, then the longest tunnel on the canal network (and where a tunnel on the Bridgewater scale might no doubt have been ruinously expensive).

Cheaper they may have been, but these narrow dimensions severely limited the volume of trade they could carry, to loads of around 30 or 40 tons per barge. This left them unable to cope with growing demand and fatally vulnerable to competition from the railways. Larger barges could operate on those canals engineered to carry them but their potential was limited by the large parts of the network that could not accommodate them.

Railways learned these lessons early on and most of them from the 1830s on (other than the more minor lines) were engineered to twin-track standard (that is, designed to accommodate two lines of tracks). One or two even had the foresight to design their bridges and other civil engineering to a four-track standard, even if it were not intended to lay four lines of track from Day 1. As for the commonality of gauge, had a later Parliamentary committee taken a more determined stand in resolving the railway gauge wars in the 1840s, generations of passengers and other rail users might have been spared the cost, delay and inconvenience of transferring from one gauge to another mid journey.

The Decline of the Canals

Inevitably most of the canals could not compete on price, capacity or speed of delivery of cargoes with the new railways and fell into a steady decline where the two came into competition. Some, like the Kennet and Avon Canal, were bought up by the railway that was taking away much of their business. The Government had a very negative view of monopolies. So when such a takeover came before them for approval, Parliament would generally make it conditional on the railway company keeping the canal open.

This was something of a pious hope. Whatever assurances were given to the government by the railway company, it can hardly be surprising that many were allowed to deteriorate to the point where, whilst still theoretically open, they were virtually unnavigable. The twentieth century saw a parallel decline in the fortunes of the railway branch lines under the competition from road hauliers and bus companies, and their eventual weeding out by Doctor Beeching and others.

7

Tracks and Tramways

While great leaps forward were being taken in locomotive design and general railway operating practices in the first thirty years of the nineteenth century, important improvements were also being made in track design. Robert Stephenson, while building the London and Birmingham Railway, made his view known that it would not be the power of the locomotives, nor their gauge, that would ultimately determine the speed of the railways, but:

> The economic endurance of the permanent way to bear the additional weight which must, as a matter of necessity, accompany every increase of speed.

We will start by looking at some of the developments of the eighteenth and nineteenth centuries, before going back into the early history of railways.

The term 'permanent way' harks back to the earliest days of mainline railway construction. Railway builders used to lay a lightweight temporary track to carry earth from where excavations were taking place to where embankments were to be formed. This track – the contractor's way – could be added to or moved as the construction progressed. When the work was complete, the tracks of the contractor's way could be lifted up and used elsewhere. Ballast would then be laid over the trackbed and the rails and other fittings of the lines that would carry the railway's traffic – the permanent way – would be laid out on it. In practice, these railways were anything but permanent, as railway engineers struggled to keep up with the pressures of ever heavier and speedier trains.

As we have seen, the earliest rails in the eighteenth-century colliery railways were generally made of wood, mounted on wooden sleepers or stone blocks. The wooden parts of the railway tended to rot fairly quickly, to a point that led some to doubt the value of investing in wagonways (or waggonways, as they used to call them). Nor were the wooden rails very able to bear the weight of loaded wagons or, more particularly, of the first steam locomotives. On a more positive note, wooden railways had a degree of flexibility that stone-mounted ones did not, leading to a smoother ride. Further problems with stone blocks included a tendency for the wooden plugs set into them for attaching the rails to get saturated, swell up and eventually crack the stone. Rails mounted on stone blocks were also more prone than those mounted on sleepers to go out of gauge and need relaying.

Initial attempts to make wooden rails more durable meant attaching an iron wearing strip along the running surface of the rail. But while these could lengthen the life of the rails somewhat, they also had a tendency to become detached from the wood. The most disturbing manifestations of this were what were called 'snakeheads' and occurred on early American (pre-Civil War) passenger trains. With these, the metal strip from the rails was propelled through the floor of the passenger carriage with sufficient force for it to go up through the passenger compartment and out through the carriage roof. One study reports seventeen cases of this happening, one of them killing an unfortunate passenger. Others were injured or had narrow escapes.

Where sleepers were used on a wooden railway that was to be horse drawn, a further practice grew up from the mid-eighteenth century of laying a 'double way', in which a second wooden rail was fixed to the top of the first. This allowed more ballast to be laid above the sleepers. This was not done to protect the horse from tripping over the sleepers so much as to protect the sleepers from wear by the horse's hooves. It also made the railway more robust, since the joints between the rails no longer had to be directly above a sleeper.

The discovery in 1709 by Abraham Darby of Coalbrookdale of a process for making iron using coke instead of charcoal resulted in a more plentiful supply of the metal. But it was either his son (also Abraham) or possibly the latter's son-in-law, Richard Reynolds, who made the first all-iron rails, in or around the 1760s. These do not appear to have been originally intended as a permanent part of the railway – they were simply a way of using up an over-production of iron at a time of economic recession – to be taken up and recast into something else once business picked up. But the new rails were found to be invaluable, more than doubling the payload their horses were able to haul.

However, cast iron also had its drawbacks. It is very brittle, and consequently could only be used for rails in short lengths (generally 3 or 6ft) which made for a very uneven ride. Even then it was still prone to breakage. The joints between the rails were the most vulnerable parts of the rail, so shorter rails meant more joints and thus a greater risk of breakage. Cast iron also cannot be bent. This meant that bends in the track could only be tackled by making a series of incremental small changes in direction from one straight rail to the next. One consequence of this was that it tended to limit the length of locomotives to two pairs of wheels, since anything much longer would not be able to ride around these irregular 'curves' without binding or falling off the rails. This small number of axles also put a heavier load on the rails, further increasing the risk of breakage. One means of trying to tackle at least one of the problems of breakages on the early tracks was the 'fish-bellied' rail. This tapered out towards the middle of the rail, to strengthen it where it got least support from the sleepers.

One partial solution to the problem came with the invention in 1812 of bogies by William Chapman. These helped to steer the locomotives around curves, and also spread the weight of the locomotive more evenly over a larger number of axles. The Stephensons had a simpler solution to the problem of binding – they omitted the flanges from the middle wheels of their three-driven-axle locomotives.

But none of these measures could make up for the intrinsic shortcomings of cast iron as a rail material. The first real breakthrough in rails came in 1820, when John Birkenshaw of the Bedlington Ironworks in Northumberland developed rolled wrought-iron fish-bellied rails. For the first time engineers had a rail that was strong enough to support the weight of a steam locomotive, even when cast in longer (15ft) lengths. But longer rails meant that they could not be supported only at the joins, and a more uniform cross-section than the fish-bellied one had to be arrived at. Wrought iron became the rail material of choice for most railway builders from then on, only being superseded by the arrival of affordable steel in the 1850s. Wrought iron also lent itself better to mass production than the cast-iron alternative.

When Joseph Locke was building the Grand Junction Railway he favoured the use of double-headed (dumb-bell) wrought-iron rails resting on timber sleepers, the sleepers spaced at 2ft 6in apart. His money-saving idea was that, when the rails became worn, they could simply be turned over and the other side used as the running surface. However, he found that the chairs into which the rails were mounted caused wear to the bottom edge, making them uneven. They were at least an improvement to the fish-bellied wrought-iron rails still being used by Robert Stephenson on the next-door London and Birmingham Railway.

The era of heavier, faster-moving traffic presented a new challenge for stone-block sleepers. With just slow-moving horse-drawn traffic there was no need for cross ties between the rails to maintain the gauge, but this was no longer the case. What was needed was a degree of flexibility, to absorb the stresses of locomotive traffic, but at the same time with the rails being held firmly to gauge. In both respects wooden sleepers performed better than stone blocks, where prolonged heavy traffic also tended to shake the rails loose. Last and certainly not least, stone blocks tended to be a more expensive option if there was no suitable quarry near to hand. When the London and Birmingham Railway decided to make the change from stone blocks to sleepers it was left with £180,000 worth of redundant stones.

Only their tendency to rot put sleepers at a disadvantage to stones, and two developments of the 1830s sought to address this. The first came in 1832, when John Howard Kyan patented a method for preserving timber. It involved immersing the timber in a highly toxic solution of mercuric chloride. While Mr Kyan spoke highly of his brainchild, the railway companies using it had mixed results. The Great Western found that six years after applying the process their timbers were as good as new. But the London and Birmingham Railways' timbers were showing signs of rot after just three years. Kyanisation fell out of favour in 1838, when John Bethell patented a creosote treatment for sleepers, applied under pressure.

There then remained the question of the weight of rail to be used – weight being an indicator of strength, and being measured in pounds (weight) per yard. This steadily grew, along with the weight of the loads the railway was carrying. For example, the Stockton and Darlington started life with rails weighing in at 28lb per yard, the Liverpool and Manchester specified rails of 35lb per yard, but by the 1840s the London and Birmingham, (along with the Liverpool and Manchester) were ordering rails of 65 or 75lb per yard for most of its tracks.

Modern railways have for many years favoured the edge rail, but there was at one time a serious rival to it. John Curr (1756–1823) was the one-time manager of the Duke of Norfolk's collieries in Sheffield, and the inventor of an L-shaped form of railway track. It was used originally for moving small wagons around underground, but came to be widely used for surface railways. One advantage was that vehicles using them did not have to have flanged wheels; any conventional road-going vehicle of the right gauge could use them and move effortlessly between rail and road. They also had rather more adhesion than edge rails, and the flanges on the wheels of edge rail wagons were brittle and prone to breakage. Against this, the L-shaped tracks tended to fill up with dirt and stones, increasing the rolling resistance, and the tracks themselves tended not to be strong enough to bear the weight of heavy wagons or, more particularly, locomotives. For some reason the colliers at Curr's mine took against these new rails and rioted, ripping them up and forcing Curr himself to go into hiding in the woods for several days, until tempers cooled. In similar vein, some railways took against steam locomotion, fearful that it might depress coal prices to an unacceptable degree.

The Ancients

But the story of railways – of one kind or another – goes back long before the developments we have been talking about. To set it in context we need first to ask 'what is a railway?' The question is not as silly as it may seem, for the earliest railways differed markedly from our modern understanding of the word. Doctor Michael J.T. Lewis, a scholar of the early railways, defines them as 'a prepared track which so guides the wheels of the vehicles running on it that they cannot leave the track'. In fact, one of the earliest systems to be covered by this definition did not use conventional rails, or carriages or wagons, and reaches far back into antiquity – to ancient Greece.

The Diolkos, as it was called, was used for transporting ships overland, across the Isthmus of Corinth in ancient Greece. This 6km overland journey saved the vessels a much longer and more hazardous sea journey around the Peloponnese peninsula. Its main function was the movement of goods, though in times of war it could also be used to gain military advantage.

The Diolkos was a trackway, paved with hard limestone and with parallel grooves set into it, running about 63in (1.6m) apart (not dissimilar to our modern standard gauge). The grooves are thought to have been deliberately cut to form guides for vehicle wheels. Archaeological evidence suggests some sort of wheeled vehicles were used to transport the boats and their cargos separately. It was also open to all-comers – at a price – making it a form of public railway (something that would not be seen in Britain until after 1800).

It could handle a considerable volume of traffic; in 220 BC Demetrius had a fleet of around fifty vessels dragged across the isthmus, and in 31 BC Octavian sent part of his fleet of 260 Linurnians (smaller galleys) across it, while pursuing Marc Anthony. But most of its business seems to have been commerce in times of peace. The main traffic was likely to have been smaller ships, but triremes (vessels weighing 25 tons and 35 metres long) could theoretically make the crossing, despite gradients of up to 1 in 16.5 in places. The largest vessels might take up to three hours to make the crossing, pulled (it is thought) by up to 180 men and animals, possibly with some help from capstans. Today, the same function is performed by a modern (1893) canal.

The Diolkos was well known in its day and had a reputation for speed; the playwright Aristophanes coined the phrase 'as fast as a Corinthian' in its honour. It functioned between the sixth century BC and at least the first (and possibly as late as the ninth) century AD – considerably longer than our modern railway system has lasted so far.

There is also some evidence of two other ancient ship trackways in Roman Egypt, one of them close to the harbour of Alexandria, though the details are scant. Fletcher and Taylor talk of tracks being found 'on the roads which lead to the ruins of the oldest towns in Latium, namely Ora, Norba and Siguia, home of the Volsci'. (Latium was a region of what is now Italy.)

The ancient Romans also appear to have used similar grooved railways. An adit at the Tres Minas gold mine in Portugal has parallel channels cut into the rock floor at a gauge of about 1.2m. No other examples of Roman origin have so far been conclusively identified in other mines, but if this one is correct, it is unlikely to have been unique. There are even rumours (no more than that) of examples, at the Douaucothi gold mine in south-west Wales, or at Blunsdon quarry in Wiltshire.

Finally, there is also evidence from ancient Persia of grooves cut into the road surface, thought to be to stop chariots tipping over on corners. Whether these were deliberately engineered or simply the product of wear is not entirely clear, but the grooves were about 4ft 8in apart. Over the centuries, traces of grooved stone tracks have largely disappeared from many areas, although the remains of a more recent granite grooved road, built in about 1826 to serve a quarry in Dartmoor, are still in existence. The Haytor Granite Roadway was built to export granite from Dartmoor (some of which was used in the construction of the 1831 London Bridge, now in Arizona). Granite was in plentiful local supply, and so was used to build some 9 miles of tracks. The quarry (and the railway) remained in use until the 1850s.

More generally, the Egyptians and other ancient civilisations were no strangers to civil engineering – and specifically transport – works, on the sort of scale that would later be needed to build the British railway network. During the Sixth Dynasty (2332–2283 BC) they built their first canals, as a means of moving the stone needed for the building of the pyramids. Considerable surveying skills were needed to maintain levels throughout its length, and they even included an early form of lock.

The Assyrian King Sennacherib, who destroyed Babylon, also built a stone-lined canal to bring water to his capital city of Nineveh in 691 BC. It was 50 miles long and as wide as a main road. Indeed, the stone floor of the canal was used as a road during the canal's construction. Its most striking features were a 300m-long stone aqueduct, carrying water across a valley, and a massive weir, used to divert water from a river into the canal, all under the stern gaze of a gigantic statue of the king.

The Chinese also had their transport engineering monuments. Their Grand Canal, part of it built in the sixth century BC, but extending over many centuries, was no less than 1,035km long. It was the most complex of the ancient world's canal systems, and was as much concerned with the irrigation of crops as with navigation. Among its features were pound locks, flash locks and slipways for changing levels between sections of canal.

Medieval to Georgian Railways

Returning more specifically to early railways, there was said to have been a stained glass window depicting an early mine railway in the Minster of Freiburg im Breisgau, Germany, dating from about 1330. But there does not seem to be much record of any railways coming into being between the end of the Diolkos and the Middle Ages. Any that appeared may have been too localised or short-lived to attract the attention of chroniclers of the period. Very small mines serving a purely local market would in any case presumably not have needed any elaborate transport arrangements. It has been suggested (but not proven) that some Cornish rutways date back to the 1550s, and were influenced by German-speaking miners working in the area.

De Re Metallica (1556), the masterwork of the German Georgius Agricola, the founding father of modern geology, contains illustrations of the guided 'hunde' carts used in some of the mines of the day. The hunde (or 'dog') carts were so-called for the noise they made while running down the tracks. These carts ran on unflanged wheels along the wooden planks that formed the mine floor, and were kept running in the right direction by a vertical pin, extending down from the wagon into a gap between the planks – stretching the definition of 'a rail' somewhat to its limits. Other types relied on the skill of the pusher to steer the wagon along a single broad plank and a third had plain wheels running in troughed wooden tracks. Any guidance a railway can provide in steering

An adit and an 11in gauge railway leading into the Goodluck lead mine, near Matlock, Derbyshire. (Ashley Dace CC SA 2.0 via WikimediaCommons)

An 1894 picture of a pit pony working an underground colliery railway.

wagons would have been particularly important in the near pitch darkness of drift mine tunnels.

A—RECTANGULAR IRON BANDS ON TRUCK.   B—ITS IRON STRAPS.   C—IRON AXLE.
D—WOODEN ROLLERS.   E—SMALL   IRON   KEYS.   F—LARGE   BLUNT IRON PIN.
G—SAME TRUCK UPSIDE DOWN.

An early colliery truck, showing (F) the primitive guidance system they used.

The West Country mining engineer Sir Bevis Bulmer (1536–1615) was familiar with Agricola's work and may have spread word of it in Britain. Another possible source of inspiration for British miners may have been Sebastian Munster's *Cosmographia Universalis*, published in 1544, part of which was translated into English by Richard Eden in 1553.

One of the earliest examples of a hunde cart operation in England was again run by Germans, but this time under royal patronage. In 1564 Queen Elizabeth I established the Company of Mines Royal as a means of exploiting the mineral wealth of some of the northern counties of England. Copper was a particular priority, being needed for making bronze for cannons, little of which was mined locally at that time. A team of German miners under one Daniel Hechstetter, an engineer from Augsburg, was appointed to do the mining, starting with a pit in Keswick, where they introduced one of these primitive railway-type structures. So again it is possible that Britain's first wagonway was the result of imported German expertise and that German miners, this time working in Caldbeck (in modern Cumbria) may have been using a wooden wagonway of some description as early as the 1560s.

British railways may therefore have their origins not in Victorian or Georgian times, but during or just after the reign of the first Queen Elizabeth, and that the main elements of the modern trackbed – a bed of stone chippings, sleepers and rails for use by flanged wheels – could have been in place by the seventeenth century. The first recorded wagonway on the Tyne dates from 1621, and certainly by 1660 there were nine wagonways on Tyneside alone, carrying coal out of the mines and down to the nearest staith (riverside transhipment point). By 1700 these railways were so widespread in the north-east that they were known as 'Newcastle Roads'. But which one is the rightful claimant to be Britain's first? Most of what we know about them comes from legal disputes, so there may be others that, having had a blissfully uncontroversial life, are lost to history. Looking at some of the home-grown candidates that we do know about:

A wagonway at Prescot near Liverpool, was completed somewhere near the start of the seventeenth century (possibly as early as 1594). It carried coal from a pit near Prescot Hall, owned by one Philip Layton, to a terminus about half a mile away.

Another was built at about the same time (October 1605) between Broseley and Jackfield in Shropshire, where a 1km railway was being used by mine owner James Clifford to transport coal from his pits to the River Severn to a point just downstream of the future site of the historic iron bridge.

A third was built between Strelly and Wollaton, near Nottingham, at some time between autumn 1603 and October 1604. It was the result of a partnership between Sir Percy Willoughby, local landowner and owner of Wollaton Hall, and one Huntingdon Beaumont (c.1560–1624), lessee of the Strelly coal pits. The 2-mile wagonway cost £172 (£37,271 in 2016 money) and the rails were made of wood. The gauge (whilst uncertain) is thought to have been around 4ft 6in (137cm), close to the 4ft 8½in (144cm) later adopted by the Stephensons. From the terminus at Wollaton Lane End most of the coal was taken by road to Trent Bridge and from there by barge along the River Trent. The railway was described (in contemporary spelling) as one of the 'new and extraordinary invencions and practices for the spedy and easy conveyance of the said coals and especially by breaking the soil for laying of rayles to carry the same upon with great ease and expedicion … and by drawing of certen caryages laden with coals uppon the same rayles'.

The Wollaton Wagonway had a relatively short life; by about 1620 all the accessible coal was worked out and this is thought to have led to it being abandoned. But Beaumont went on to build further wagonways for his other mining interests near Blyth, Northumberland, and is said to have introduced the wagonway to the north-east. Beaumont's wagonways may have been the first in the region, but arguably the most important was the Tanfield wagonway (discussed later in the chapter).

A typical *modus operandi* for a wagonway linked to a mine might be as follows. It would normally be a downhill route from the pithead to the riverside staith, where the coal would be loaded onto barges or larger ships. On the steeper parts of the descent (which could be as steep as 1 in 15) the horse would be detached from the front of the wagon and would walk behind it. (Some later mines even gave their horses the luxury of their own wagon, known as a dandy cart, in which they could ride downhill.) Meanwhile, the driver would attempt to control the rate of descent with a brake lever on which he sat, and which acted on two of the coal wagon wheels. This was not without its dangers. In wet weather the braked wooden wheels would lose virtually all their adhesion on the wooden rails. In these circumstances, some mines would employ boys to scatter sand or ashes onto the rails to restore some semblance of grip.

On reaching their destination, the wagons would be unloaded into barges and the horse would pull the empty trucks back up to the pithead. A variation on this might be to have a gravity arrangement – twin tracks, with the wagons linked by ropes to a pulley at the top, so that the weight of the loaded wagons going downhill pulled the empty wagons back up to the pithead.

The geology of the coal-bearing areas had an influence on the detailed design of the railways. In the north-east most pits had vertical shafts down to the coal measures, so railways were not used until the coal had been lifted out of the mine onto the surface – hence the wagons they used could be relatively large scale and with a broader gauge. They would tend to run on wooden rails, since the brittle cast-iron ones would tend to break under the weight of a fully loaded wagon of this size. But in the Coalbrookdale area of Shropshire many of the mines were drifts, running into the hillside at a shallow angle. This meant that the railways could be taken right up to the underground coal face. The wagons had to be smaller and narrower gauge to operate underground, and with less stress on the wheels, cast-iron wheels were more of a realistic option. This may help explain why, in the first third of the nineteenth century, north-east railways nearly all changed over to edge rails (which could bear the weight of large wagons), while the Shropshire collieries were much more likely to go for more lightweight plateways to carry their smaller wagons.

An early more detailed description of a wooden colliery railway survives from 1765. In this, the rails were planks from dismantled ships, about 7in high by 5in wide, mounted on cross sleepers at 2 or 3ft intervals. Their gauge could be anything from 3 to 5ft. But they had a relatively short working life and were prone to breaking. As we saw, it became common practice to lay a thin strip of iron as a running surface along the top of the rails. This lengthened their working lives somewhat and reduced rolling resistance for the horses. But it also increased the wear on the wooden wagon wheels and led to the introduction, from the mid 1700s, to the introduction of iron wheels, which wore better but at the cost of being harder on the rest of the trackbed. The iron wearing surface on the rails was still not enough to stop them buckling under the weight of the wagons.

Gauge

How was the standard gauge for British railways arrived at? Many of the key formal decisions, such as the Gauge Act 1846 and the removal of the last vestiges of Broad Gauge in 1892, fall well outside of our timescale, but the topic was one of considerable interest well before 1830.

The Stephensons based the standard gauge of their early railways to a large degree upon the dimensions of the horse and the load it could pull.

This in turn had (to varying degrees) dictated the dimensions of farm and other horse-driven vehicles throughout the ages (including early mine railways). Any vehicle much larger than 5ft in width (or gauge) would tend to overburden the horse, whereas anything much smaller would not make full use of its pulling power. This rule of thumb applied to railways long before the Stephensons – unsurprisingly, given that most of the early railways were horse-powered. Even the Stockton and Darlington Railway was designed with modified horse-drawn vehicles forming part of its traffic.

Looking back even further, archaeological investigations in Pompeii and elsewhere in the 1870s established that the Romans' common wagon gauge was almost exactly 4ft 8in, which is calculated from the ruts in the roads caused by heavy use, which are thought to be just that – ruts, and not deliberately engineered steering grooves. This was all very well for a horse-drawn railway, but how relevant was it for a steam railway? In some respects 4ft 8½in is not a bad fit to the dimensions of human passengers. It enables two humans to sit in comfort side by side, with room for other passengers to pass by them (though modern carriage interiors are rather wider than the gauge of the rails, and tend to take three or four passengers abreast).

But there were those among the railway designers who felt that 4ft 8½in was less than an optimal gauge for a steam railway. Science suggests that a steam engine gets more efficient, producing its output at a lower average cost, as it gets bigger than the standard gauge would accommodate. A broader gauge format would also allow a larger boiler, and for it to be mounted lower, making the locomotive more stable. Apparently most early railway engineers favoured something between 5ft and 5ft 6in, to give them extra room for a larger boiler and to achieve a lower centre of gravity.

With an L-shaped plateway, an external edge to external edge measurement of 5ft would give you something very close to Stephenson's 4ft 8½in, when measured from the internal edges of the track.

George Stephenson himself, according to Faith, confessed that he had originally favoured a 5ft 2in gauge, but had been persuaded by his son to keep to 4ft 8½in (1.435m). The first railways to be built by the Stephensons and others tended to be widely separated from each other, but Stephenson had the foresight to realise that one day they would be joined together, in a single national network. To do so, their gauges would all have to be the same. Stephenson (perhaps inspired by William James) gave notice of this early in his career. Working simultaneously on the railways at Killingworth and Hetton, Stephenson was at pains to ensure a common standard at both.

Despite this, the early iron railways around the country varied greatly in their gauge. They could be 2ft or less in mountainous areas or underground, around 3ft 6in or 4ft 2in on plateways and 4ft or more on edge railways. The 1778 edition of *Encyclopedia Britannica* maintained that 4ft was 'the common gauge' for many early railways and certainly a number of them chose 4ft, including the Redruth and Chasewater (Cornwall's first public railway – approved in 1824), the Padern in north Wales (1841–42) and the original Kilmarnock and Troon (1805). But many railways opted for something else. The Surrey Iron Railway was thought to have had a 4ft 6in gauge, while the Penydarren ran on a roughly 4ft 4in tramway, while the Middleton was 4ft 1in. Many south Wales lines were built to a standard of 3ft 6in or less, whilst most pre-1835 Scottish lines were 4ft 6in (or 6½in). Two exceptions to the Scottish rule were the Dundee and Arbroath and the Arbroath and Forfar (both approved in 1836, at 5ft 6in) while three English lines followed the example set by William Hedley at Wylam Colliery and went for 5ft 0in.

But the greatest challenge was to come from Isambard Kingdom Brunel and his Great Western Railway. As Christopher Awdry said, and we have seen, Brunel was not flying in the face of convention when he proposed his 7ft ¼in broad gauge, because there was at that time no real convention to fly in the face of. Up until then most individual engineers tended either to follow local tradition or their own personal preferences in setting a gauge. Brunel could at least offer a rational basis for his broad gauge. He explained to his shareholders that the standard gauge tended to limit the size of the carriage wheels and raise the centre of gravity of the carriages, making for a rougher ride and more wear and tear on the wheels. He wanted to have the wheels of his rolling stock of a larger diameter, so that they would revolve more slowly, with less wear and danger of overheating.

The only way this could be done without making the rolling stock absurdly top-heavy and potentially unstable was to have the wheels outside the main body of the carriage or wagon. This could not be done and still leave enough usable space in the carriage or wagon with a 4ft 8½in gauge, or with the next step up – 5ft 6in. A further increase, to 6ft 6in, apparently raised a potential problem with derailments on crossovers, leaving Brunel with his 7ft ¼in broad gauge. The extra ¼in, like the ½in Stephenson added to his standard gauge, was to allow for smoother running, without binding, on bends. Brunel managed to secure a Parliamentary consent for his railway that made no mention of the gauge, leaving him free to pursue his preferred option.

As an aside, it should be added that Brunel's father, Marc, worked in Chatham Dockyard between 1808 and 1812, where they used a broad-gauge railway to carry logs to a sawmill. It had an unorthodox method of fixing down the rails that was not unlike that used by the Great Western in its early days. It is not known for certain, but likely, that father and son discussed this railway.

Looking farther afield, Ireland's railways had so many different gauges that they only arrived at a standard one by taking an average. In the United States, railway gauge was sometimes taken as a symbol of state independence. There were initially eleven different gauges among the northern states and anyone travelling between Philadelphia and Charlestown might at one stage have experienced at least eight changes of gauge. For more than half a century Australia's two largest cities – Sydney and Melbourne – were separated by a change in gauge.

Brunel also had his own ideas when it came to laying the track. The Stephensons laid the rails for many of their early railways directly onto stone blocks, which they felt gave the track a desirable rigidity. (In fact, they proved to be too rigid for the railways' good.) They later (as horses gave way to steam) opted instead for transverse wooden sleepers. Brunel had a more sophisticated and more expensive – a hefty increase to the tune of about a £500 a mile – option, though he insisted it would more than pay for itself in maintenance savings. Certainly it gave the Great Western a much smoother and more stable ride than many of its competitors. This involved laying 30ft longitudinal timbers along the entire length of the railway. These were bolted to cross timbers at about 15ft intervals. These cross timbers stretched across the two lines of track and all four rails were bolted to them. Within the two lines of rails of each track piles of beech were driven into the ground and bolted to the cross timbers.

A replica of Brunel's unorthodox broad-gauge track layout, seen at Didcot Railway Centre.

The piles were intended not to support the timbers, but to hold them down. To prevent the weight of the trains cutting into the timbers, a wedge-shaped strip of hardwood was laid between rail and timbers.

Engineering, Sleepers and Stones, Tram Plates and Edge Rails

One or two of the earliest British railways included civil engineering on an ambitious scale for the day. The Causey Arch of 1726 – the world's first railway bridge – had a span of 150ft (46m), the largest bridge span in Britain at that time. It cost £12,000 to build. The Tanfield Waggonway (1727), the railway of which it was a part, was at its peak carrying 450,000 tons of coal a year, the equivalent of one wagonload every forty-five seconds. At more than 8 miles long and linking several mines to the River Tyne, the Tanfield Waggonway was also one of the longest horse-drawn railways in the country as the steam railway age grew near. By this time, a broad consensus seems to have been reached that the maximum economic length of a horse-drawn wagonway was about 10 miles.

The Tanfield Waggonway was built in the 1720s by the Grand Allies, a group of immensely wealthy north-east coal mining families who were seeking monopoly control of the London coal market. (From one of these, Sir George Bowes (1701–60), the late Queen Mother and hence Queen Elizabeth II are descended.)

It ran from collieries near Blyth to a shipping point on the River Tyne at Redheugh. Most of the area's earlier wagonways had been fairly basic affairs (wooden tracks running wooden-wheeled trucks) but this was a much longer and more heavily engineered operation. It would give the Grand Allies collieries a dominant market position, from 1725 until the line's final closure in 1964. The oldest part of this railway therefore predates the Middleton, but the latter bases its claim of primacy on the fact of it being the first to secure Parliamentary approval.

No mention has so far been made of ballast. Railway tracks using sleepers are underlain by ballast. The quantity varies with the amount and nature of traffic the line was carrying. By the end of the nineteenth century lines carrying express services needed 1700 cubic yards of ballast per mile (around 105,000lb weight) and minor (third-class) tracks 600 cubic yards per mile, making the railways a major customer for the quarrying industry. Ballast aids drainage and helps spread the load over the ground beneath the tracks. It can also help prevent vibration causing structural damage to trackside buildings, and a deeper layer of ballast is needed where this could be a potential problem.

In the early days, all sorts of unsuitable material such as blast furnace slag, ash from industrial fires, seaside gravel, mineworking spoil, railway clinker or even small coal was used as ballast as an economy, leading to longer-term problems. Some ballast arrived as a consequence of the delivery of coal to its destination. Colliers returning to the north-east after delivering their coals to London would need to have some weight (or ballast) in their cargo holds to keep the ship stable in a rough sea. This could take the form of stone chippings, which the railway companies could then use for railway-building purposes.

But ballast has to be the right kind of stones and many of these were not. Rounded stones are unsuitable as railway ballast, as they tend to slip out from under the sleepers too easily. Ballast made of sharp-edged stones is much better at interlocking and staying in place. Today crushed hard rock such as basalt or granite is used. Even with modern cleaning techniques (and cleaning is essential if ballast is to continue to do its job effectively) it has a limited life and the modern British rail network needs 3 million tons of fresh ballast a year.

For those choosing blocks to mount their rails, the choice between wood and stone blocks could depend upon the local availability and cost of stone. On the Stockton and Darlington Stephenson used stone for that part of the route nearest to a quarry, and wood (from old sailing ships) for the rest. As we saw, the stone blocks would have holes bored into them, into which a piece of wood could be inserted for fixing the rail. Tie bars would be needed at intervals to maintain the correct gauge. Blocks were the norm until the 1830s, when sleepers became more commonplace. As well as being better at holding the rails together at the correct gauge, sleepers also distributed the load from the rails more evenly over the ballast and helped give a less bumpy ride. Stone blocks were more prone to vibration and splitting.

8

The Role of Parliament

In this chapter we look at the role of Parliament in vetting proposals for the early railways, and in controlling them, once up and running. Here, perhaps even more than in some other parts of the book, we will breach our self-imposed time frame in the interest of providing a joined-up narrative.

We saw elsewhere how the Middleton Collieries of Leeds got Parliamentary consent to build a wagonway, linking their collieries to a waterway, where the coal could be transhipped into barges. Obtaining Parliamentary approval for a railway scheme in Britain could be a complex, lengthy and extremely costly business. No other country had such expensive procedures. For some railways, the cost of obtaining Parliamentary approval could be greater than that of actually building the line. For example, the promoters of the Great Northern Railway spent £433,000 (this in the currency of the day, not a modern-day equivalent) obtaining Parliamentary approval. This was over and above what their supporters and opponents spent. After the Liverpool and Manchester Railway received Parliamentary approval, at what the Great Northern Railway might have regarded as the bargain-basement price of around £70,000, there were calls for a review of the system:

> The moment a scheme that is likely to be beneficial to the country is proposed, it is treated as a public nuisance by the Parliament … as a general offence against the nation, which is only to be expiated by a huge tax.
>
> *Monthly Review*

A public bill gives rise to legislation that applies to everyone within its jurisdiction, whereas a private bill applies only to an individual, group of individuals or corporate body, such as a local authority or public company. A private act can grant relief from other laws, a unique benefit, grant powers not available under the general law or give relief from the legal responsibility for some otherwise unlawful action.

If the capital to construct a railway was to be raised by public subscription, and/or its course was to lie across public land or that of individuals not associated with the scheme, a private Act of Parliament had first to be obtained. There were two reasons for this. First, as the law of the time stood, joint stock companies, such as would be needed to raise the finance for the scheme, could only be set up either by Royal Charter or a private Act of Parliament. Second, an Act of Parliament was needed to ensure that the scheme proceeded in accordance with whatever terms Parliament laid down. For example, this might involve the compulsory purchase of land, without the owner's consent but paying fair compensation. It might involve crossing public highways, diverting rivers and streams, fencing off railway lines or setting up schemes of arbitration where land values were disputed.

There were other reasons why a Private Parliamentary Bill might be needed; for example, if a communal right of way were to be taken over by a private body such as a turnpike road or a new railway. Local transport needs might be given priority over the national legislature and powers created, for example, to enable the compulsory purchase of land, or for tolls or fares to be collected. The process was not without its flaws. Local needs might be correctly assessed but national interests disregarded, or vice versa.

The Process

The first stage in the process was for the promoters to advertise their intentions in the official newspaper of record – *The London Gazette* – and in any other newspapers whose circulation areas were likely to be affected by it, so that legal challenges could be mounted where necessary. The next step was to deposit a petition at the Private Bill Office, with a series of documents explaining the purpose of the scheme, the names of the petitioners, its costs and benefits (and to who they would accrue), the specific powers required to implement the bill and how it was to be funded. It was to include a ground plan of the project, including a list of the landowners and other interests that would be affected by it. Submission of these papers had to be done according to a strict timetable – within fourteen days after the first Friday after the opening of the Parliamentary session – if proposals were to be considered in the next session of Parliament. Copies also had to be posted with the clerks of the peace in the counties through which the railway intended to pass. All this copying was in itself a major undertaking in the days before photocopiers and other sophisticated reproduction techniques were invented.

The years of 'railway mania' are full of stories of clerks working round the clock to get their submissions prepared in time, post-chaises (the 'fast cars' of their day) waiting at the railway-company door to effect a rapid delivery to Parliament, staff fighting with each other to get through the doors before the deadline, not to mention skulduggery to prevent their rivals making their delivery on time. Parliament was itself overwhelmed and in the peak year of 1846 so many parliamentary committees had to be set up to review them (more than 700 in that one year alone) that temporary wooden huts had to be erected outside Westminster so there was somewhere for them all to meet.

By the time the next railway mania overcame the nation (1864–67) Parliament would have a rather less disjointed approach. Faced with 257 proposals for underground railways in and around London in 1864, the two Houses of Parliament formed a joint committee, which advised against many of them, and instead proposed the creation of what is now the Circle line.

Each of the Houses of Parliament had its own standing orders for drawing up and presenting private railway Bills, with which applicants had to comply. These had been drawn up between 1774 and 1797, and were based on those for navigation (canal) bills. If it cleared that hurdle a bill could be drafted and given two readings in the House of Commons, seven days apart. The Commons could then either refer it to a committee for more detailed consideration, or send it back to the promoters.

The committee stage was where the minute scrutiny would take place. Supporters and opponents of the scheme would be questioned – not just by members of the committee, but also by lawyers and others representing a host of interests, and the committee would then vote on whether to commend it to Parliament, amend it or reject it outright. There was no shortage of material for the witnesses to go at; the bills could be substantial documents (that for the Liverpool and Manchester Railway ran to 101 pages, for example, before account was taken of the 150 or so petitions opposing the scheme, which also needed to be considered).

Promoters needed detailed knowledge of Parliamentary procedures and legal requirements and a Parliamentary agent was invariably recruited. This was a man with legal training, accredited by Parliament, with a team of solicitors and barristers to support him. Until 1810 this had been done by an officer of the House of Commons (and recharged to the petitioners). It had then been 'privatised', as the volume of bills had led to the creation of a Private Bill Office. It was staffed by teams of Parliamentary agents employed by specialist private legal practices. They were as much interested in the precise terminology of the bill and whether this conformed with accepted usage, and with adherence to timetables, as they were with the merits of the scheme or the competence of the petitioners. More generally, the Parliamentary agents acted as a go-between between the petitioners and Parliament.

Also in great demand were 'celebrity' engineers – top railway builders such as the Stephensons, Brunel, Locke, Rennie and a handful of others, whose name on a survey as 'consulting engineers' gave it instant credibility. A top engineer could earn 100 guineas (£105) a day as an expert witness in front of a Parliamentary committee. Robert Stephenson was one who over-committed himself, lending his name to no fewer than thirty-four applications for bills. Over and above this, in a single morning he received unsolicited cheques totalling more than £1,000. These Stephenson returned with the message that 'their evidence was not a power to be bought and sold'. To their credit, George Stephenson and Brunel were two of the premier league of surveyors who resisted any endorsement of a scheme in which they were not genuinely involved. Even so, Brunel found himself appearing before Parliament (or one of its committees) on

233 occasions. Railways accounted for much of the 5 million pages of evidence now held in Parliamentary archives, and the 200,000 appearances by witnesses between 1771 and 1917.

Parliament tried to streamline the committee process for dealing with Private Members' Bills. The committees were reduced from mobs of about twenty Members of Parliament, many of whom had a local interest in the outcome, to four or five Members with no personal or constituency interest in the outcome, and who were supposed to act quasi-judicially.

Parliament was the sole arbiter of railway schemes, which ranged from the sound to the downright corrupt. But Parliament was itself riddled with vested interests bordering on corruption. As Robert Stephenson's biographer, John Cordy Jeaffreson, put it:

Peers and Members of the Lower House were avowedly engaged in traffickers in the railway market ... Members attached to 'the railway interest' voted for each other's projects ... there was in those years scarcely a person in the House of Lords or in the House of Commons, who was not, personally or through his connections, anxious that a Bill should be obtained for some particular new line.

In 1845 a total of 157 Members of Parliament had their names on the registers of new railway companies. One company alone was able to boast the support of 100 votes in the House of Commons. Peers were in even greater demand. Two members of the House of Lords were directors of twenty-three and twenty-two railway directorships respectively. Apparently, even the Lords Spiritual, the Bishops who occupied seats in the House of Lords, were not immune to this ungodly temptation.

The railway approval process was not a new one. As we saw, Parliament approved its first railway bill in 1758 (the Middleton Railway), and the act for the Stockton and Darlington Railway was the twenty-first railway act to be approved by Parliament. This was over and above the many parallel processes undergone in the peak years of canal building.

On most of the earliest railways, it was not necessary for the act to specify the means of motive power – it was either men (or more likely) horses. Only as they entered the nineteenth century did a further option become a possibility. The first Stockton and Darlington Act did nothing to resolve the ambiguity. Worse, the Earl of Shaftesbury, the chairman of this House of Lords committee, did not have a clue what this 'loco-motive' thing referred to in the Bill was and had it struck from the bill. But the promoters had to come back to Parliament to agree some route changes, and took the opportunity to clarify matters. The bill was unopposed, but George Stephenson and his team still had to travel to London to explain to the Earl of Shaftesbury what a steam locomotive was. George was scathing in a letter to his company solicitor, Francis Mewburn:

> Lord Shaftesbury must be an old fool. I always said he had been a spoilt child but he is a great deal worse than I had expected.

Spoilt child or not, the idea of steam locomotion thus entered the statute book in the following – less than ringing – words:

> … it shall be lawful for the proprietors to make and erect such or as many loco-motive or moveable Engines as the said Company shall from time to time think proper and expedient and to use and employ the same upon the same Railways or Tramroads or any of them, for the purpose of facilitating the transport conveyance and carriage of Goods, Merchandise and other articles and things upon and along the same Roads, and for the conveyance of Passengers.

Over and above all the private member activity, there was also public legislation on railway matters, such as safety, charges for traffic, accounting and telegraph wires and so on. The Railway Clauses Act 1835, for example, specified the minimum headroom for different classes of road going under or over a railway line. One of the most important early examples of this legislation was the Regulation of Railways Act 1844, which was prompted by an early railway disaster in which eight people were killed in a crash at Sonning, near Reading, on Christmas Eve, 1841. William Gladstone, then President of the Board of Trade, saw it as an opportunity to bring the railways under better control. But the many railway interests in Parliament, who christened Gladstone's unwelcome draft legislation the 'Railway Plunder Bill', thought otherwise.

As originally drafted, the act would have given Parliament control over the fares of any railway company that paid a dividend of more than 10 per cent a year over a three-year period, and given Parliament the right to buy any future railway fifteen years after its incorporation. It would also have provided for the cut-price transport of troops, the poor and the insane, among other provisions. The bill was savaged by Parliament and by a public in the grip of a 'get rich quick' railway fever, and in private by the Prime Minister. The main good to survive from it was the so-called Parliamentary Train, which provided affordable travel for the poor. This required every railway to run at least one train a day, along the full extent of its lines and in both directions, stopping at every station, for a fare of no more than a penny a mile. Passengers were to have seats, weather protection and free carriage of up to 56lb of luggage, and the train had to average at least 12mph, including stops.

In its first full year, 4 million passengers travelled by Parliamentary Train.

The Railways and Competition

> There is a wholesome absence of interference in this country in all those matters which experience has shown might wisely be left to private individuals stimulated by the love of gain and the desire to administer to the wants and comforts of their fellow men.
>
> John Bright MP, Hansard 1844 xxvi

As we saw, the first public steam-hauled railway, the Stockton and Darlington, based its modus operandi on the model of a turnpike road, having nothing more pertinent on which to model its operation.

But the laissez-faire rules of the highway did not work on a railway. A railway is something that lends itself to monopoly; there had to be one operator. Many in Parliament came to realise this as well as the general public, but monopoly was anathema to many of its Members. This coloured the way in which the Parliamentary process for approving railways worked in Britain. Whilst competition may not be a big issue for colliery railways transporting coal from one pithead to the nearest river, it was a different matter if the line were a public railway, part of a network joining two or more centres of population.

If free competition and anarchic public access along a given length of line could not work, one alternative might be competition by having more than one railway serving the route between A and B. This helps to explain how Britain ended up with so many duplicated routes. Little consideration was given to establishing a rational and efficient national network. Instead, rival routes could find themselves in a price-cutting war in which neither party could make a reasonable profit. Samuel Laing, Secretary to the Board of Trade, summed this up to a Parliamentary committee:

> Competition is more efficient as an instrument of injury to existing companies than a means of guaranteeing cheapness of travelling ... The public have never permanently benefited from competition between different lines of railway.
>
> Quoted in Hylton, 2007

As for the railway companies, there was a good deal of confused thinking, much of it motivated by self-interest:

> There was ... much confusion in the minds of the railway directors. The representatives of the existing companies said they did not want 'dangerous meddling' from the Government – and then complained bitterly that the Government did not prevent the construction of competitive lines which 'destroyed' the capital of the original lines. Then again, when railway companies amalgamated to reduce competition and improve their efficiency, they were accused of 'monopoly' by parliament and public.
>
> Vaughan, 1997

The European Model

It is instructive to compare all this with the way the matter was approached in different parts of continental Europe, as word of Stephenson's success with the Liverpool and Manchester Railway spread. The paths followed by some other nations are detailed in a later chapter. But of the British railway proposals, the Liverpool and Manchester Railway attracted some of the strongest opposition of any scheme – unsurprising, perhaps, given the importance of the centres that it was connecting. Many of the sources of opposition were predictable; rival means of transport, such as canals, stagecoaches and turnpikes; inn-keepers along the coaching roads and the landed gentry who foresaw (or feared) that the railway would intrude into their estates; not to mention:

> ... the subversion of the vested interests in property of various descrip-
> tions – by the depriving of the labouring classes of the community of
> employment – by the barrier which it will create between those parts of the
> country which it will intersect, and by a train of other evils too numerous
> to particularize.
>
> Birmingham Gazette, 7 February 1831

The Railways and Democracy

One further hurdle railway proposals would have to overcome was the fact that not everyone was enamoured with the idea of railways in principle. War hero and Prime Minister the Duke of Wellington was concerned that they would encourage the working classes to move about unnecessarily, thereby contributing to the spread of subversive ideas. In his capacity as Chancellor of the University of Oxford he managed to prevent the Great Western Railway coming within 10 miles of the dreaming spires for a number of years.

In similar vein, the Headmaster of Eton strived mightily for years (though ultimately with limited success) to prevent the railway coming anywhere near his college, fearful that it might whisk his pupils off to the depravities of London. Benjamin Disraeli, in his satirical novel *Sybil*, has one of his characters complaining about the railways having 'a dangerous tendency to equality', reflecting a view prevalent in his day. Last but by no means least, eminent critics such as John Ruskin objected to railways, not least because of what they saw as the unpleasantness of the environment through which one had to travel – the railway station:

> It is the very temple of discomfort and the only charity that the builder can
> extend to us is to show us, plainly as may be, how soonest to escape from it

... It transmutes a man from a traveller to a living parcel. From the time
he has parted from the noblest character of his humanity for the sake of a
planetary power of locomotion.

The Seven Lamps of Architecture, 1849

There was also nimbyism and snobbery. Doctor Arnold, headmaster of
Rugby School, initially welcomed the coming of the railways as the
potential destroyer of feudalism, then opposed a railway scheme that
would harm the view from historic Turweston House. He was joined in
this last view by Squire Stratton, the longstanding Mayor of Turweston,
though their views on feudalism differed sharply. The squire apparently
thought feudalism was a splendid institution. His nightmare scenario
was of hosts of railway workers coming into the town. Few would be
locals; most would come from the north of England; they would speak
in horrid accents and live in row upon row of back to back houses,
encased in smoke and soot.

The Steam Locomotive

But there was one new line of attack for opponents to the railway by
the early nineteenth century – the steam locomotive. Its use on the
Liverpool and Manchester Railway was far from clear-cut. It was only
finally resolved after the Rainhill trials of 1829, and after the railway
itself had won Parliamentary approval in principle. But as early as 1825
the promoters of the railway had commissioned trials of steam locomotives at Killingworth Colliery. Killingworth was, of course, the one-
time workplace of George Stephenson, the great champion of steam
locomotion, and Stephenson had been appointed engineer to the
Liverpool and Manchester Railway.

There were good grounds for steam locomotion becoming one of the
battlegrounds of the committee. As we saw, up until then, Bills had tended
to be silent on the subject of motive power, or had specified that they
would be horse-drawn. The Stockton and Darlington had been the first to
have steam locomotion written into their enabling act, and this only in an
addendum to a follow-up act, agreeing some changes to the route.

Early railways used hand signals to control trains. Every mile or so along the line a railway policeman in his sentry box (its correct name is 'police station') attempted to maintain a reasonable time interval between services. This one is preserved at the Didcot Railway Centre. (Author's collection and *Illustrated London News*, December 1844)

Stephenson and his colleagues were well aware of the potential attack on locomotives, and Stephenson was advised to play down the possible speed of them, lest this frightened nervous would-be passengers into opposing the scheme altogether. Health scares also featured large among the reasons for opposing locomotives, and they were not helped by so-called 'experts', such as Dionysius Lardner, Professor of Natural Philosophy and Astronomy at the new London University, who informed his readers in 1824 that:

Rail travel at high speed is not possible because passengers, unable to breathe, would die of asphyxia.

from *The steam engine familiarly explained and illustrated*

This was by no means the only accusation laid at the door of the steam locomotive, which the Mayor of Liverpool summed up as 'the vilest nuisance that ever the town had experienced' (quite a claim, given what we know about living conditions in these and other Victorian industrial towns and cities). Dealing first with just the physical impacts on the passengers, a Member of Parliament claimed that a fifteen-minute train ride had left him with a serious headache and the notion of instant death. Pregnant women were warned that they would miscarry and those that were not pregnant would be made barren; babies would be born deformed and passengers suffocated in tunnels due to carbonic acid exposure; colds, catarrh and consumptions would become commonplace, as would weakening of the heart and brain and premature ageing.

It would cause those inclined to it to suffer 'suicidal delerium [*sic*]' (that is, of course, were their lives not first imperilled by the lunatics or smallpox victims that would doubtless be sitting next to them). Later, a rumour spread that excess speed was bad for the eyes. A doctor had to be found by the railway company to reassure the public through the pages of the *Liverpool Mercury* that even speeds as high as 34mph would 'cause no inconvenience or alarm nor would the eye be disturbed while viewing the scenery'.

Other damage would be more widespread across the community. The locomotives' 'long and black trains of smoke would destroy lawns, orchards, fields, saloons and hot-houses, and stop cows giving milk'. It would stop animals grazing and hens laying; country inns would close and birds would be killed in mid-flight by the smoke; farmland would be destroyed and farms and other buildings burnt to the ground; foxes and pheasants eradicated and foxhunting prevented; horses would be extinguished as a species and oats and hay become unmarketable. Anyone surviving this Armageddon would no doubt be carried off by the next boiler explosion.

As we can see, most of this was arrant nonsense, and was seen as such by the Parliamentary committee. But the process did bring up some more telling criticisms of steam locomotion. The management of the Stratford and Moreton Railway found, based on some tests carried out (admittedly in 1821, early in the development of steam locomotion), that steam railways required much heavier and more expensive tracks than their horse-drawn equivalents; that they could not pull an adequate load up a 1:72 gradient and were not noticeably faster than a horse-drawn vehicle on the flat. They were also much more liable than a horse-drawn vehicle to explode (though this was often a product of the driver's folly in locking the safety valve down, rather than a fundamental problem with steam locomotion).

Then there was the question of speed, which excited fear even among many would-be supporters of steam. In 1825, just as the first Liverpool and Manchester Bill was struggling to make its way through Parliament, Nicholas Wood, manager of the Killingworth Colliery and friend of George Stephenson (someone who might be expected to be a champion of steam power), wrote in his *Treatise on Rail-Roads*:

> It is far from my wish to promulgate to the world that the ridiculous expectations, or rather professions, of the enthusiastic speculists be realised, and that we shall see them travelling at the rate of 12, 16, 18 or 20 miles an hour; nothing could do more harm to their adoption, or general improvement, than the promulgation of such nonsense.

During the Liverpool and Manchester Parliamentary hearings Stephenson was warned by his counsel not to overstate the case for (or perhaps report the truth about) steam locomotion in his presentation to Parliament – in particular not to mention 'insane' speeds like 20mph, or 'he would be regarded as a maniac fit for Bedlam and damn the whole thing'. Brunel was given similar advice for his Great Western presentation. In the event, Stephenson talked of speeds of 4–8mph, merely hinting at the speculation that much more was achievable. He was able instead to put the emphasis on the economies possible from steam locomotion, based on the experience of the Stockton and Darlington line – where locomotion, stationary engines and horses were all employed.

The Liverpool and Manchester Railway petitioners lost the first round of their Parliamentary battle, and George Stephenson (temporarily) lost his job as chief engineer as a result. But they would try again, this time with a team more highly qualified and plausible (if not more experienced) and with answers prepared for more of the questions that would be posed of them. On 5 May 1826 a bill was passed 'for making and maintaining a Railroad or Tramroad from the Town of Liverpool to the Town of

Manchester'. Steam-hauled railways had passed into a new age. As one chronicler put it:

> There was a world of difference in building a colliery railway from coal-fields [such as the Stockton and Darlington line] and constructing a line to link the principal port of Liverpool with the great manufacturing centre of Manchester.

With the Rainhill trials and the Parliamentary process leading to the Liverpool and Manchester Railway Act, steam railways had faced – and passed – some of the sternest tests of their legitimacy. That was not to say that the battle was conclusively won. It took until 1839 for a Parliamentary committee under Sir Robert Peel to recognise the special characteristics of railways and to grant all new ones a monopoly of haulage rights. Even so, Section 42 of the Railway Clauses (Consolidation) Bill 1845 still allowed for the possibility of new railways being made subject to the old-fashioned turnpike principle.

9

Railways and the Industrial Revolution

At the same time as the infant railway network was taking shape, Britain was undergoing its own, wider transformation. Fundamental changes in the mechanisation and productivity of agriculture and in a whole range of industrial processes were taking place, in which the railways would come increasingly to play their part. But the Industrial Revolution's impact did not stop at the farm or factory gate – it heralded a whole range of wider social, cultural and economic changes. The railways' impact on these had only just started to be felt by the cut-off point in our narrative, but it would grow to enormous importance over the half century that followed. In this chapter we will look at some of these changes, and see how, from small beginnings, the railways would help to create the modern industrial world. First, the transport dimension to the Industrial Revolution:

The Transport Revolution

In the mid to late eighteenth century Britain was in the grip of not one, but three transport revolutions. The year 1761 is generally taken as the starting date for the Industrial Revolution, with the opening of the Bridgewater Canal, Britain's first wholly artificial canal, and its dramatic impact on coal prices in Manchester. This would lead to a period of frantic canal building in the 1790s, forerunner to the railway mania of the 1830s and '40s, in which railways would come to play an increasingly important subsidiary role to the canals themselves, before eventually superseding the canals entirely.

At first the railways and canals co-existed quite happily, with the railways providing less-expensive feeder routes to the canal network, but the Duke of Bridgewater was one who saw the longer-term threat that the railways posed to the canals, in providing cheaper and quicker transport. As he said shortly before his death in 1803, 'They (the canals) will last my time, but I see mischief in those damned tram-roads.'

The opening of the Bridgewater Canal coincides closely with a landmark in a second transport revolution – the Parliamentary approval of the Middleton Railway in 1758, the first railway to receive this official blessing, through a process that was to become the way forward for all the national railway network.

The third revolution – in road transport – started rather sooner, after centuries of neglect going back to post-Roman times. This period of neglect included centuries in which each parish was supposed to maintain its part of the road network but generally failed to do so. In about 1680 John Ogilby produced a map, showing how far a traveller on horseback might get in a given time on Britain's roads as they were at that time. He concluded that London to Birmingham took just over fifty hours, while London to Manchester was around 100.

The first turnpike (toll road) appeared in 1663. By 1750 some 150 were in place around the country, but the latter part of the eighteenth century saw some of the most intensive periods of turnpike building. A further 400 were established between 1750 and 1772 and the start of the nineteenth century saw the total exceed 700. By the 1830s virtually all the country's trunk roads and many cross-country routes were turnpiked.

At their peak, more than 1,000 turnpike companies looked after 20,000 miles of road and it undoubtedly made a big difference to many long-distance journey times. London to Edinburgh, a journey that a century before could take a fortnight by stagecoach, could by 1830 be done in two days, and the London to Manchester journey time fell between 1700 and 1787 from ninety hours to twenty-four (including overnight stops). Between 1750 and 1800 average stagecoach journey speeds increased from 2.6 to 6.2mph, and that average grew to 8mph by 1829. By then, the very fastest stagecoach services were averaging around 10mph. This was the speediest thing on the roads in its day, but *Rocket* at Rainhill was already achieving three times that speed, and by the end of the 1830s the fastest express railway services would be claiming speeds well in excess of 60mph.

That said, there were still in 1813 some 95,100 miles of road that were not turnpiked or paved. Moreover, turnpiking was itself by no means an automatic guarantee of a smooth, well-maintained road. A Government-commissioned survey of the condition of the nation's turnpikes in 1838 showed that almost 40 per cent were classified as 'bad', 'not good' or 'tolerable' (bearing in mind that this was the trusts themselves being asked to evaluate their own roads, so hardly the most critical of assessors).

Even if the stagecoaches had been able to speed things up further they had just about reached the limits of what they could deliver, given that they remained a horse-drawn industry. For the first time, the speed of travel along the turnpike network was constrained by the capability of horses, rather than the state of the roads. Steam road vehicles were not the answer, for they were extremely expensive to run on roads. This was despite the road-going steam coaches of the likes of Walter Hancock and Goldsworthy Gurney being capable of 20–30mph by 1830. The turnpike tolls for them could be up to fifteen times those charged for a comparable horse-drawn vehicle, largely due to the damage they allegedly caused to the road surface (the real extent of which was in fact questionable). Finally, mention should also be made of some of the individuals in this period who sought to improve the quality of road building.

Jack Metcalf, blind from the age of 6, had almost supernatural powers to build good roads without being able to see them. In a career that only ended with his death at the age of 93 he built some 180 miles of high-quality turnpike, mostly in his native Yorkshire. Then there was John McAdam, who introduced the word 'Macadam' to the English language (the 'tar' part of his methodology came later). He developed his own construction technique for road building, which bought him into conflict with another leading civil engineer of the day, Thomas Telford. But both men saw public enthusiasm for their road improvements fizzling out with the coming of the railways.

But even if stagecoach journey times could have been further reduced, the cost of road travel and its limited carrying capacity meant that stagecoaches remained an elite, minority form of travel. Mass public transport of any kind by road only started to happen from the late 1820s onwards, when omnibuses started to be introduced to some of our major cities – but these were still horse-hauled, only for short urban journeys and in their early stages were hardly 'mass transit'. Finally, any hope steam-powered road traffic might have had of competing with the railways would in the longer term be well and truly knocked on the head by the Locomotive Act 1865, (the so-called Red Flag Act). This imposed a speed limit of 4mph on rural roads and 2mph in towns for steam vehicles, and required them to be preceded by a pedestrian carrying a red flag.

A fully loaded stagecoach of the type soon to be superseded by the railways.

In the event, the stagecoaches were some of the first businesses to suffer from the competition of the railways. The London to Brighton route probably had as well-developed a stagecoach service as any in the country, with hourly departures and a journey time of five hours or less for the 56-mile (95km) journey. As for price comparisons, before 1830 a return stagecoach trip between London and Manchester would cost around £3 10s (£3.50). By 1851, the railways had dramatically reduced the cost of the same journey, as well as making the journey swifter and more comfortable. The stagecoaches could not compete in any respect and would be put out of business within a couple of years of the rival railway service opening (which in Brighton's case was in 1841). Some of those operators were at least able to find new business, supplying shorter feeder services to the railway stations.

More generally, the improved speed and lower cost of delivering people and goods by railway meant that a whole new range of goods and services suddenly became available and affordable, new, previously distant places became accessible and new ways of conducting business and spending one's leisure emerged.

Industrial Revolution

A number of criteria needed to be met to provide the seedbed for an Industrial Revolution. We will look at just a few of these, in particular ones in which the railways had a role.

Manpower. One requirement for an Industrial Revolution is an increasing population that can be directed into industry. In addition to the increased population resulting from improvements in health care and nutrition, a substantial new labour force was being released by the revolutions that were taking place in agriculture, science and technology, displacing agricultural workers from the land and craft workers from their traditional employment. A sizeable part (300,000 at its peak) of this labour force would find its way into the construction of the canals and the railways. From 1815, peace with the French would also free up a large demobilised former military workforce.

Yet others would find their search for new employment aided by easier access to new labour markets. This was made possible by the railways, especially after the cheap 'Parliamentary trains' became available (by 1870, 67.9 per cent of all the nation's passenger journeys would be made by third-class or 'Parliamentary' travellers).

Raw materials: Plentiful raw materials were needed, ideally in close proximity to each other, where this was necessary for manufacturing purposes. For example, medieval England was rapidly exhausting its supply of woodland by its competing demands for timber, until the increased use of coal for domestic heating eased one pressure on timber supplies, and Abraham Darby eased another by his development of a coke-smelting technology for the production of iron, replacing charcoal. Unfortunately, the supplies of these raw materials generally tended to be far removed from the main markets for their manufactures, places like London. It would take the transport revolution provided by the railways to help 'shrink' the distance between the places of extraction and manufacture, and the marketplace.

Urbanisation: Adam Smith was one of the founding fathers of economic theory and his book, *The Wealth of Nations*, set out some of the basic principles that would underpin the Industrial Revolution. It was published in 1776 and therefore pre-dated the railways becoming a major force in the land. But several of his insights are of relevance to the railway age. In particular, his views on the advantages of canals over other forms of transport for the movement of goods with a high weight-to-value ratio would later apply with even greater force to the railways.

Smith said that there were some industries that could only be carried out in 'a grand town'. Elsewhere, the market for them is too narrow. Someone living somewhere with a limited market would find it harder to enjoy the benefits of division of labour, since the market for their finished goods would not be big enough to support all the individuals involved in their production. Such individuals would be forced to become less-productive generalists. So urbanisation was an essential prerequisite for the Industrial Revolution. In 1750, just 15 per cent of Britain's population lived in towns or cities. By 1800, the total population had grown substantially and 25 per cent of them were classed as urban.

Urbanisation was also needed to make possible the concentration of population and scale of manufacturing that made the application of steam power a viable proposition. Water power, on which many of the earliest factories relied, was unreliable and not always available in locations and quantities that met the other needs of the factory system. It has been suggested that one of the driving forces behind the development of steam power was the growing shortage of suitable locations for water-powered development.

But if the population of an individual urban area did not grow, an alternative was for existing settlements (and their industries) to be given access to wider markets, courtesy of radical improvements in transport. Either way, the railways had a vital role to play in creating Smith's 'grand towns'.

The canals serviced the earliest stages of urbanisation, but sustained urbanisation on the scale seen in England throughout the nineteenth century would only have been possible with the railways, to import the amounts of food, fuel and other needs of the growing urban population, to supply the raw materials their factories needed for production, and to deliver the fruits of their labours to a wide enough market to make the enterprise viable. There must be serious doubt as to whether the alternatives to rail – canal and turnpike – could have sustained anything like Victorian levels of growth in the longer term. In fact, when it came to making the first application for Parliamentary approval, the Liverpool and Manchester petitioners were advised (by Sir John Barrow, Second Secretary to the Admiralty, no less) to build their whole case around the inability of the canals and roads to service the growing urban areas.

To take the example of Manchester, those alternative modes of transport were already creaking in the early stages of industrialisation. The Liverpool and Manchester Railway was a scheme born out of merchants' profound frustration with, in particular, their canals. They were slow, costly and inefficient, and it used to be said that it took longer to get cotton from Liverpool to Manchester than it took to ship it all the way from America. Merchants would attract fines from the dock company for the extended periods their goods lay undelivered on the quayside. As for the needs of the resident population, uncertainties over food supplies led to food riots in Manchester in 1762, 1795, 1796 and 1800.

In addition to urbanisation, the railways and commuting also made possible the prospect of suburbanisation – of people no longer having to both work and live in the centres of our towns and cities, with their overcrowding, squalor and pollution. This is not to say that the railways' role as an unofficial town planner was always a benign one. All other considerations aside, railways swallowed up vast swathes of urban slum property for their tracks, stations, engine sheds and marshalling yards. The railways singled out slum property as the cheapest and least controversial land to acquire for their developments. Just one building – London's St Pancras station – involved the loss of 4,000 homes, which were generally not replaced. This forced many inner-city inhabitants (those who could not afford the luxury of commuting) to seek ever more squalid and overcrowded accommodation in such cheap property as remained in our towns and cities. In many Victorian towns and cities the railways swallowed up at least 10 per cent of the land in their central areas.

Monopoly, competition and regulation: One topic on which the railways and Adam Smith (along with much public opinion of the day) parted company was their attitude to monopoly, as opposed to free competition – an important question for the early railways. Smith was strongly opposed to monopoly, and saw free competition as an important driver for industrialisation:

> Monopoly … is a great enemy to good management, which can never be universally established but in consequence of that free and universal competition which forces everybody to have recourse to it for the sake of self-defence.

And again:

> The price of monopoly is in every occasion the highest which can be got. The natural price, or the price of free competition, on the contrary is the lowest which can be taken, not upon every location indeed, but for any considerable time together.

Governments of the day were similarly averse to monopoly, and, as we have seen, the Act approving the first public steam railway (the Stockton and Darlington Railway, 1821) anticipated it operating on the turnpike system applied to toll roads. That is, that anybody with the right gauge of wagon to fit the tracks (and with the toll money) could turn up and use the railway, regardless of the rolling stock's condition, safety considerations, technical competence of the operating staff, timetabling, volume of traffic or more or less anything else. In the chaos that followed the opening of that railway and the operation of these principles, it became clear to most people that railways tended towards a monopoly – with a single organisation being needed to take charge of locomotives and rolling stock, management, training of the train crews and the hundred and one other considerations that go to running an efficient (and safe) railway line.

The authorities then reasoned that if individual railways could not deliver free-market competition among its customers, perhaps two or more companies competing for the same custom could drive up standards while driving down prices. Thus even quite modest urban areas could, courtesy of successive laissez-faire governments, find themselves served by two or more railway lines provided by different companies (Brighton had six potential railway suitors at one time). But all too often this arrangement could lead to a price war, from which none of the parties could prosper and even passengers could be disadvantaged by penny-pinching economies, as the companies tried to gain the competitive edge. As we will see in Chapter 10, some other countries did not suffer from these problems.

One final form of control was through regulation – again, something that did not come easily to early nineteenth-century governments (especially when dealing with such large and powerful pressure groups as the Parliamentarians who declared a financial interest in railways).

Time and timekeeping. Mention must be made of one other way in which railway-led change made its mark on industrial Britain. The increasing pace of life in an Industrial Revolution society made accurate timekeeping ever more important. Before the railways, there was no nationally established basis for setting the time. It was done locally, based on the rising and setting of the sun – or God's time, as it was known. This did not allow for seasonal variations in the earth's orbit around the sun, or for the sun being lost behind clouds at key times. More to the point, the sun rose and set at different times, depending upon where the observer was standing. For points due north and south of each other this was not an issue, but to the east and west was a different matter.

To take an extreme example, the sun rose almost half an hour earlier in Yarmouth than it did in Penzance. It could therefore be difficult
catching a train if your watch was set to one form of local time and the
engine driver's to another. In stagecoach days, your progress was sufficiently leisurely for this to be less problematic, but as the rail network
grew and connections became more critical, some form of uniformity
was unavoidable. The problem became absurd in places such as Rugby
station, where one platform ran London and North Western Railway services (working on local time) while another was used by the Midland
Railway (London time). This became an issue from the opening day of
the Liverpool and Manchester Railway in 1830 (which runs east–west),
though the time differences there were relatively small, the journey from
Liverpool to Manchester being short. Nonetheless, that railway had
standardised to GMT (Greenwich Mean Time) at both ends of its route
by 1846.

The railways generally were to lead in a national campaign to
standardise on GMT, after the Great Western adopted it in 1840.
Various outposts of inconsistency remained until the Astronomer
Royal started transmitting GMT signals around the country from the
newelectro-magnetic clock at Greenwich, but it was not until 1880
that the Definition of Time Act made GMT the nation's legal basis for
timekeeping for all purposes, not just railway times. Four years later the
rest of the world followed suit and GMT became the world's basis for
conducting business.

The railways would eventually become one of the most heavily regu-
lated areas of economic activity. By 1856 Robert Stephenson was able to
claim that there were 186 separate pieces of legislation pertaining to the
London and North West Railway alone, though how effective many of
these were, he felt, was open to question. They were trying to control some
unwilling organisations – like those railway companies who would prefer
to continue paying out compensation to the families of victims killed
in rail accidents, rather than spend money on safety measures that could
have prevented the accidents in the first place. More generally, regulation
became accepted as an appropriate activity for many areas of government,
and Victorian England would also see the introduction of inspectorates of
factories, mines, schools, among other bodies.

The railways and democracy. Modern Britain is a democratic state, but until 1832, the election of governments was an activity reserved for the privileged and tiny minority who were eligible to vote. Worse still, in many constituencies, even this electorate were either virtually non-existent or were given little or no choice of candidate. These were the voters in what were known as 'rotten boroughs' (constituencies with just a handful of electors) or 'pocket boroughs' where the choice of MP rested with a single landowner (who could evict, threaten or bribe any elector/tenant he saw voting 'the wrong way' in the non-secret ballots of the day).

At the same time, major cities and towns such as Manchester (population in 1831 182,000) had no Parliamentary representation at all. The new-found mobility of the railways threw these iniquities into sharp relief. The Liverpool and Manchester railway line, for example, went through the rotten borough of Newton, which had just fifty-two registered electors, and two Parliamentary seats, which were in the control of the Legh family. Thousands of rail travellers passing through the area must have wondered at the logic of such an electoral process, and added fuel to the pre-existing pressure for change. Within two years of that railway opening, the Reform Act of 1832 widened the franchise and started the nation along the long road to universal and equal Parliamentary representation.

Finance. The Industrial Revolution also needed a stable and favourable financial regime, with reliable banks and a class of people who were willing to invest in industry (and, in particular, provide the unprecedentedly large sums required by the railway industry). We have been seeing some of the ways in which the coming of the railways facilitated the Industrial Revolution, but there is also evidence that the Government's changing financial rules gave the railways an advantageous position in securing funding.

Following an earlier spell of speculative madness by the investment market (the South Sea Bubble), the Government passed the so-called South Sea Bubble Act (1720). This forbad the formation of Joint Stock companies, unless authorised by Royal Charter or Special Act of Parliament. By the nineteenth century this act was proving to be an obstacle to industry and investment, and it was repealed in 1825. This led to several other banks emerging, operating on the joint stock principle.

Railways, having been set up under private Acts of Parliament, were thus allowed to register as joint stock companies. This meant that railway shareholders were protected by limited liability – that they could not be held responsible for any company losses beyond the sum they had already paid for their shares (or rather beyond the face value of their shares, if they had acquired them on the basis of, say, a 10 per cent deposit). Investors in railway shares therefore did not need to feel that they were putting everything they owned at risk (unless, like some, they had speculated everything they owned on railway shares). Limited liability for many other companies had to wait until the Limited Liability Act (1855) and the Joint Stock Companies Act (1856). It helped make railway shares a favoured vehicle for investors, second only to the security offered by Government stocks. But Government stocks paid at best 4 per cent, whereas shares in, say, the Liverpool and Manchester Railway, offered dividends at or near 10 per cent. With some of the earliest railway shares looking like a licence to print money, it was small wonder that they became so popular.

Communications and the spread of ideas. The circulation of ideas was important to the Industrial Revolution and the railways had an important role to play in it. Until the railways there was no such thing as a national newspaper as by the time a daily newspaper reached the farthest flung corners of the kingdom, its news was often no longer very current. From the very earliest days the railways took over the national distribution of newspapers, with the result that most of the nation could be reading the same (subversive) ideas on the same day.

In similar vein, human spreaders of disaffection became much more mobile and pressure groups such as the Anti-Corn Law League were quick to take advantage of the railways to get their orators and their pamphlets before a much wider audience. The introduction of the penny post within a few years of the first railways was also instrumental in spreading ideas and was greatly assisted by the railways becoming to a large degree the nation's postman. Finally, there was the introduction of the telegraph system, which used the railway routes as the highway for their telegraph poles. As well as

From the earliest days of rail, mail delivery was transferred from stagecoach to railway. Here one of the last mail coaches (from Louth) is leaving Peterborough, bound for London by train. (From a painting by James Pollard, 1845)

the railways using the telegraph for operational purposes, the new technology also made it possible for news to be transmitted instantaneously from one end of the country to the other.

The Railways and the Industrial Revolution

So how important were the railways to the Industrial Revolution? For the years in which we are particularly interested, perhaps not as important as is sometimes thought. They really started to come into their own from the 1830s. Before that, they were relatively few in number and unconnected, and therefore suitable only for short-distance travel, or to meet the particular needs of their individual promoters. Apart from the obstacle course of securing Parliamentary approval to build the line, the controls exercised by the authorities over railways, once built, were relatively limited in effect (if numerous).

But by 1830 the seeds had been sewn, the potential demonstrated. Ideas such as a national railway network, built to a common gauge and operating standards, were beginning to form in people's minds. From 1830 the growth of the railway network would be swift and dramatic, so that by 1840 there was already the skeleton of a national system in place or under construction.

The potential for the canals and road transport to continue sustaining the growth of the industrial revolution was limited by the low-speed, high-cost and limited capacity of the services they provided. Britain would have been a very different place, had it needed to rely on the roads and the canals as its main arteries of communication throughout the nineteenth century. But what was important to the fledgling railways were the years of technological expertise and practical experience that their pioneers had accumulated, allowing the full potential of the railways to be appreciated and built upon, from the 1830s and throughout the nineteenth century.

The Pleasures of the Rail-Road. — Caught in the Railway!

Opponents of the early railways forecast chaos in their wake.

10

Supplier of Railways to the World

The early progress of steam-powered locomotion in Britain was closely followed throughout the world. Leading British locomotive and railway builders would receive visits from foreign delegations – either of the technical kind, or of senior politicians or members of their Royal Families; as we saw, among the crowds at the 1829 Rainhill trials were a number of senior railwaymen from different countries, eager to see what the 'most improved locomotive' of the day looked like and how it performed.

Britain would soon be exporting its expertise and best practice throughout the world and its influence continues to this day. If Stephenson's *Rocket* were in full running order today, it would still be able to pass through the Channel Tunnel and run on much of most of the European network and beyond, such was Britain's early influence and its longevity. In the rest of this chapter we will look at the earliest days of some of those nations' railway development and the ways Britain's experience influenced it. We will start with the nation that, within a decade of 1830, would have built half of the world's railways.

United States of America

The United States was only slightly behind Britain in its development of steam transport, though its development followed some rather different routes. At the start of the nineteenth century, the settlement of the USA was largely confined to the eastern seaboard. Beyond it lay vast areas that were largely unexplored and uninhabited (apart from its indigenous inhabitants). Much of the nation was separated from the inhabited part by mountain ranges, great rivers and lakes. Early settlers concentrated their attentions on these waterways and one of their early modes of transport were 'flat boats'. These were extremely crude, unpowered, home-made rafts, that were floated downstream with the river currents and, once their cargo had been delivered, were broken up and sold for lumber. The first of these flat boats was sailed by a Pennsylvania farmer named Jacob Yoder, from Illinois to New Orleans in 1782, taking three months at an average speed of 3mph. It was the first of many, but their role was necessarily limited, not least because most of the western rivers flowed north to south, whereas what was most needed were east–west routes.

The steamboat era was said to have begun in 1811, when Nicholas Roosevelt, great grand-uncle of future President Theodore Roosevelt, sailed the steamboat *New Orleans* from Pittsburgh to the city of New Orleans. By 1826 more than 200 steamboats were estimated to be in operation on the western rivers, but their operation was not an unqualified success. Competition between ambitious skippers meant that accidents were commonplace. Charles Dickens, in America in 1842 and about to book a river journey, was advised to get a berth towards the aft, 'because steamboats generally blew up forward'. Road travel meanwhile had made little advance beyond the building of some turnpikes, some of which were little better than the tracks they replaced. Where there were not conveniently routed rivers to travel along, canals would often be built. Thanks to some heroic feats of engineering, some of these canals wound over timber aqueducts and through impenetrable forests, linking river to river. By 1832, Ohio alone had more than 800 miles of canal and the United States as a whole several thousand.

Some Early American Railway Lines

The New Jersey Railroad Company was the first railway in America to be chartered, in February 1815, but it was not the first to begin operating. It planned to build a railroad from the River Delaware near Trenton, to near New Brunswick. However, the investors failed to materialise and it was never built. The idea would emerge later (1832) as the Camden and Amboy Railroad (C&A), but the primacy (it was chartered in 1828 and the first 12-mile phase opened in 1830) belongs to the Baltimore and Ohio (B&O), which was also, by most reckonings, America's first common carrier railroad.

It was built because the city of Baltimore (in 1827 America's third biggest) wanted to compete with the newly completed Erie Canal, serving New York City, and with another proposed canal serving Philadelphia and Pittsburgh. It was 200 miles nearer to the western frontier than New York but, despite this, Baltimore would face economic decline if it did not have its own route to the western states. A group of twenty-five local merchants and businessmen met in 1827 and masterminded the idea of a railroad, with its potential for leapfrogging ahead of their rivals and their slower, water-based transport routes. The choice of a railway was an easy one, since the range of hills to the west of Baltimore was high enough and steep enough to make a canal a non-starter. They were led by two businessmen, Philip Thomas and George Brown, who had spent 1826 in Britain, seeing how railways operated there. Their proposal met with huge local approval; it was over-subscribed and it was said that virtually every citizen in Baltimore bought a share. The first phase of the B&O ran from Baltimore to Sandy Hook, entirely within the state of Maryland, but it was steadily extended, until the rail company could boast that the railway 'linked 13 Great States with the Nation'.

Another innovation was the B&O's part private sector, part state and local government management structure. This gave rise to some interesting policy tensions, with the private-sector directors favouring the maximisation of profits and dividends, whilst the local government appointees wanted low fares and all construction costs being funded from revenues.

Railway engineering was in its infancy when work started on the B&O, and they erred very much on the side of sturdiness, making everything they could (even the trackbed) out of granite. However, granite proved to be too unforgiving and too expensive for the purpose, and a number of the B&O's stone bridges proved surprisingly prone to being put out of use by floods. One that survives is the B&O's first bridge, the Carrollton

Stephenson's first locomotive supplied to American customers, in 1828. Its original name was *Pride of Newcastle*, not *America*.

Viaduct. This is now the second oldest railway bridge in the world still carrying traffic, preceded only by the Skerne Bridge in Darlington (England), which dates from 1824–25.

Unlike Britain, with the opening of the Liverpool and Manchester Railway in 1830, it is difficult to identity a single starting point for the American Railway Age. The development of the American railways needs a more detailed account than we have space to give it, and we will have to satisfy ourselves with a few of the firsts (or disputed firsts) claimed for American railways, up to or around our cut-off date of 1830.

One of the world's earliest railway tourism offers is to be found in the Mauch Chunk and Summit Hill Railroad, carrying its passengers up to what was described as the 'Switzerland of America'. The station at the summit was one of the first to host travellers and they continued to receive tourists from 1827 to early 1932. This tourist attraction doubled as an anthracite railway, and was worked by a combination of gravity and horse power.

One claim for the first rails to be laid in America was a 3-mile length of track at Quinsey, Massachusetts, dating from 1826 and worked by horses, but a great many other coal and mineral railways were also established during the 1820s. An earlier claim for primacy may be a 1-mile wooden gravity railway, used for the transport of gunpowder at Falling's Creek, Virginia, in 1811. Earlier still was Thomas Leiper's railroad, opened in 1810 to transport stone from a quarry in Delaware County Pennsylvania to Ridley Creek and the Delaware River.

The Baltimore and Ohio Railway laid claim to being the first steam-powered railway in the United States to be chartered as a common carrier of freight and passengers, in 1827. It also boasted the first passenger and freight station (Mount Clare, 1829), the first American railway to collect passenger receipts (December 1829) and the first to publish a timetable (May 1830).

But the Granite Railway in Massachusetts began operating in 1826, and it too has been called the first commercial railway in the United States, since it was the first to evolve into a common carrier without an intervening closure. However, its original function was as a quarry railway, linking pithead to navigable water, albeit incorporating some new features such as points and a turntable. It went through timber, granite-topped, iron-topped and then solid iron rails in the search for the best running surface.

There have been various claims to have been the firsts to use steam locomotion. For this purpose we will exclude John Stevens' 1825 'garden railway' (see later), since it was not part of any commercial enterprise.

At this stage America lacked most of the infrastructure needed to support railway building, and items such as locomotives and rails generally needed to be imported from Britain. The very first steam locomotive to run on American rails was therefore a British import, *Stourbridge Lion*, in 1829, though it was withdrawn after its record-breaking (but more importantly track-breaking) trial run on the Delaware and Hudson Railroad. It never saw commercial service. The locomotive's chequered history is outlined elsewhere in the book.

The first American-built locomotive to run (moderately) successfully in the States was *Tom Thumb* (1830), built in just six weeks by Peter Cooper of New York, weighing less than 1 ton and using musket barrels for boiler tubes. This was not intended as a serious commercial venture, but rather was a demonstration of the feasibility of steam locomotion on the first phase of the hilly B&O line. This was in part a response to Robert Stephenson, no less, who had discouraged the use of steam locomotion on the line, fearful that it could not navigate the tight bends. As part of its promotional campaign, the railway company staged a race between *Tom Thumb* and a horse. Unfortunately for public relations, *Tom Thumb* broke down and the horse won. But it did enough to demonstrate that steam was a possible option to power the route. The company later held its own version of the Rainhill trials to find a suitable locomotive for its needs. It was won by the locomotive *York*, built by Phineas Davis of York, Pennsylvania, which became the first locomotive in regular service.

The South Carolina Canal and Rail Road Company was chartered in 1827, with a core business of hauling bales of cotton. When completed in 1833 it was for a time, at 137 miles (220km), the world's longest railway. It also lays claim to be the first American railway to use steam locomotives 'regularly' (whatever that term means). It was also a railway built in part by slave labour. The company leased enslaved labour from plantation owners when white labourers refused to work in the swamps. The need for a railway arose when the city of Charleston started losing business to a number of canals, transporting cotton from the growing areas to

Coalbrookdale, where the first iron rails were made – seen here at night. (Philip Jacques de Loutherbourg, 1740–1812)

Tom Thumb, an early American-built locomotive bought in to test the viability of steam traction on the Baltimore and Ohio Railroad. This is a 1927 replica of the 1830 original. (Library of Congress)

navigable rivers. The canals, for their part, were suffering from delays, mishaps and droughts.

The first American-built locomotive to enter commercial service was *Best Friend of Charleston,* built by the West Point Foundry of New York for the South Carolina Canal and Railroad Company and brought into scheduled use in 1830. *Best Friend* met a gruesome end in June 1831, when the fireman tied down the safety valve to stop it making a noise. The boiler blew up, killing him. The locomotive was fit only for salvaging spare parts, which were used in the building of another locomotive, *Phoenix.* Public confidence in steam locomotion had to be restored by putting a wagon piled high with bales of protective cotton between that locomotive and the passenger carriages as a safety barrier.

Then there were the state firsts. On 9 August 1831 the Mohawk and Hudson Railroad's locomotive *De Witt Clinton* (named after the recently deceased Governor of New York who had commissioned the rival Erie Canal) became the first steam locomotive with real fare-paying passengers to operate in the state of New York: it was the fourth steam railway to operate in the United States. Its coaches were initially made of

Modern replica of the *Best Friend of Charleston*.

stagecoach bodies and the locomotive itself only lasted until 1833, when it was scrapped. A replica was built for an 1893 exposition in Chicago, and was frequently used thereafter promote the railway.

One further claim, this time for building what was said to be the first 'indigenous American-type locomotive' (presumably a reference to items such as the wheel arrangement, with a four-wheel bogie at the front) goes to J.B. Jervis and the Mohawk and Hudson Railroad in 1832, for its locomotive *Experiment*. The purpose of the bogie was to help prevent the locomotive derailing and to share its weight more evenly over a number of axles, since the tracks in America were often built with a minimum of preparation of the ground, and were consequently uneven. The bogie (apparently suggested to Jervis by Robert Stephenson) helped to cancel out imperfections that might derail locomotives that would have been perfectly stable on English tracks. For the same reason, American locomotives were characterised by flexible underframes, which again helped iron out any unevenness in the rails.

A rival claim to antiquity, but this time coupled to longevity, comes from a British import, *John Bull*. It was built by Robert Stephenson and supplied to the Camden and Amboy Railroad of New Jersey – an earlier locomotive

John Bull, built by the Stephensons for the Camden and Amboy Railroad in 1831. Note the adaptations for American track conditions. (Library of Congress)

De Witt Clinton as it would have appeared in its inaugural run in 1831. (Library of Congress)

of the same name had previously been tried on the Mohawk and Hudson, where its weight wrecked their insubstantial rails. It first ran on American soil in September 1831. It is now owned by the Smithsonian Institution and became the oldest operative locomotive in the world when it was fired up for a one-off display in 1981 for its 150th birthday. *John Bull* was built in Britain, but modified by C&A staff to incorporate all the features we now associate with vintage American steam locomotives – a lead bogie, cow-catcher, covered cab, headlight, bell and a covered tender.

An American Railway Hero

If Messrs Thomas and Brown were local heroes in Baltimore, America also had its own father of the nation's railways, as it were, an American George Stephenson (albeit without quite the same technical background). This was John Stevens (1749–1838), a New York-born lawyer, inventor and all-round steam enthusiast. He it was who in 1803 built a steamboat with a multi-tube boiler and screw propeller. He helped secure America's first railway charter (the New Jersey Railroad Company) in 1815; built the first American steam locomotive railway (in 1825, though only as a recreational feature in his extensive garden); and was involved in a host of other inventive schemes.

Another link between John Stevens and American steam was through the Camden and Amboy Rail Road (C&A – successor to the aforementioned New Jersey Railroad Company of 1815, of which his son Robert was president in the 1830s and 1840s). They were in direct competition with the Delaware and Raritan Canal Company in trying to link Philadelphia and New York City – the one with a canal and the other with one of the new-fangled (for 1830) railways. The C&A was one of the first (or possibly even the first) to have passenger traffic as a major part of its business plan. It aimed to compete with the stagecoaches running between New York and Philadelphia.

The Americans engaged in a huge amount of railway building during the 1830s. During that decade more than 3,300 miles of railways were built (compared with 2,000 miles of canals). By 1840 the United States had built more than half of the world's railways and by 1850 it had the world's largest network, with a greater mileage than England and France combined. The scale of their railways' growth illustrates the massive size of the labour force required to build it and helps to explain why American railways were much quicker than their British counterparts to use steam shovels and other technology to do so. It is worth mentioning that, as in Britain, American railway schemes were vigorously opposed by vested interests who saw their businesses threatened by the new mode of transport. Also as in Britain, some of the allegations were nonsense, claiming that railways were a 'device of the devil' and could cause 'a concussion of the brain'. As with so much else, railway builders looked to England for guidance on how to build a railway, in terms of gauge, how to construct a trackbed and the limits to curvature and gradient.

But the American railways' greatest days were to come after the time period on which we are focusing, with the epic crossing of the continent and the pivotal role the railways played in the American Civil War. The southern states concentrated their pre-war efforts mainly on short lines, linking cotton growing areas to navigable waterways. The lack of a strategic network would tell against them in the hostilities that were to follow.

Germany

Germany did not exist as a united state until 1870, which makes it difficult to talk about early German railways and, in particular, about state involvement in the development of a national railway network (since there was no single state). However, as we have seen in earlier chapters, the use of wagonways connected with the coal industry in what became modern Germany suggests that evidence of their use pre-dated the British experience. When Queen Elizabeth I wanted to develop a new mining industry in 1564 she turned to German expertise to set it up and run it. And, as we also saw, at much the same time (1556) the German Georgius Agricola produced his illustrated guide to operating a wagonway, in *De Re Metallica*.

By 1787, a 30km network of wagonways along the River Ruhr linked the collieries to the riverside loading bays. It was all horse-drawn and with no public access, but some of them already had iron rails, from which came the German word for railway – *Eisenbahn*, or 'iron way.'

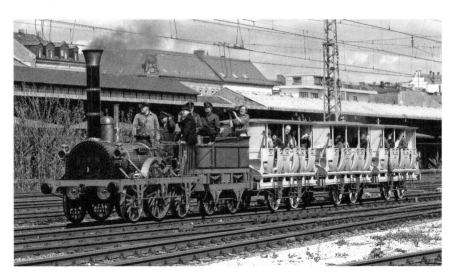

A replica of Germany's first locomotive – *Adler* – one of the British Patentee class, built by Robert Stephenson and Company. (Magnus Gertkemper CC SA 3.0 via Wikipedia Commons)

There was a lot of interest in Germany in the progress of the first British steam locomotives (Trevithick in 1804 and Blenkinsop in 1812), and in the first public railway between Stockton and Darlington. Attempts were made to catch up and overhaul the British; Johann Friedrich Krigar made a copy of the Blenkinsop engine at the Royal Iron Foundry in Berlin in 1818, and another to serve a coal line in the Saarland. These were not wholly successful, but far-sighted businessmen could already see the potential in them. Lined up against them was a curious alliance of ordinary working people, who feared for their livelihoods with the advent of these machines, and the innate conservatism of the ruling classes, as typified by this comment about horses and trains from King William I of Prussia:

> No one will pay good money to get from Berlin to Potsdam in one hour when he can ride his horse there in one day for free.

The aristocratic class tended to prefer costly and prestigious (but economically inefficient) canal schemes to railways. But there was also a growing middle class that saw railways as being of benefit to society, not to mention a good investment for their savings.

The 1830s were difficult for German railway builders, hampered as they were by having to deal with up to three dozen (often tinpot and conservative) little states and with complicated arrangements for land assembly. But despite this, by the 1840s the major cities in the future Germany were linked by rail, albeit that the responsibility for the service was fragmented between states.

Initially the Germans lacked the technological skills to be a major player in the industry and relied on engineering skills bought in from Britain. In many areas the acquisition of railway engineering skills would be the catalyst for developing a wider technological skill base. But it would not be until 1838 that Germany produced its first home-built locomotive, *Saxonia*.

The motivating factors behind the growth in importance of railways were somewhat different in Germany to those in Britain. Britain had been a single identifiable unit ever since the Act of Union with Scotland in 1707 (as England had been for centuries before that); Germany was still in the process of unification under Prussian leadership, and the development of national identity was important to them. Rapid and easy communication between one part of the emerging state and another was an important part of this.

The opposite side of that same coin was the ability to move one's armies to the appropriate part of the national frontier quickly, to resist threats from any of their continental neighbours. Nineteenth-century Britain faced no corresponding land-based threat from their neighbours, and had for centuries put their trust in the seas that surrounded them and the Royal Navy for their defence. In nineteenth-century Britain one of the main military functions of the railway was not foreign threats, but to get the army within easy reach of disorderly parts of the domestic working-class population at times of civil unrest.

A couple of early horse-drawn (and in some cases wooden-tracked) railways were built in Germany between 1820 and 1831. One, the Deirthal Railway (later named the Prince William Railway) was principally for transporting coal, but from 1833 included some passenger wagons 'for enjoyment'. It was also in 1833 that the economist Friedrich List published his plan for a German national railway network.

But the scheme that really heralded the era of modern railways in Germany is generally taken to be the Bavarian Ludwig Railway. Just 4 miles long, it was built in 1835 by the private Ludwig Railway Company and ran between Nuremberg and Furth. It was very much a celebration of British technology. Its first locomotive, named *Adler*, was built by Robert Stephenson and Company (one of its Patentee class), and was driven by an Englishman, William Wilson, who became something of a local celebrity. Germany also adopted all British standards relating to rail profile, track gauge, flanges, wagons, and so on. Moreover, the rest of the German railway network followed the same set of standards as it was developed. Oddly enough, this line never became part of that network and finally closed down, to be used as a tramway, from 1922.

The first section of the Leipzig–Dresden Railway opened in 1837, between Leipzig and Althen. It was the third German railway to be built, the first long-distance line (75 miles or 120km) and the nation's first exclusively steam-powered railway.

Thereafter the lines followed in rapid succession:

- The Berlin–Potsdam railway with its extension to Berlin was the first railway in Prussia and opened in stages in 1838;
- Also in 1838 the Duchy of Brunswick State Railway opened between Brunswick and Wolfenbüttel. It was Germany's first state-owned railway, presumably publicly funded to stop Prussia buying it up, but it did so anyway when the Duchy got into financial trouble;
- A third line opened in 1838 was the Düsseldorf–Elberfeld Railway, serving the Rhineland;
- The Taunus Railway, linking Frankfurt and Wiesbaden, the capital of the Duchy of Nassau, opened in stages between 1839 and 1840.

A host of other lines, many of them long distance, opened in the 1840s. By 1845 Germany already had more than 2,000km of railway lines and by 1855 that number had grown to more than 8,000km. Most of the states had publicly owned railway companies, but there were also some large private ones. Among these latter was the world's first international line, the Rheinische Eisenbahn, completed in 1843 and linking Cologne in Germany and Antwerp in Belgium. This grew into a genuine European network by 1859, when the French and Belgian networks and German lines west of the Rhine joined up with a central European one that reached (among other places) Prussia, Galicia, Hungary and Trieste in the

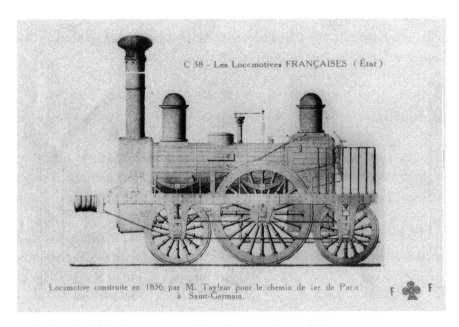

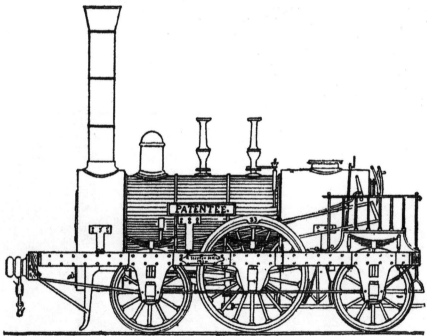

Patentee, a Stephenson locomotive type chosen in 1834 to launch the Belgian and French railway systems.

Mediterranean. By the following year the first junction had been established with the Russian railway.

Belgium

In places such as Belgium (newly independent of the Netherlands following the revolution of 1830–31) and Germany (moving towards unification under Prussian influence) worries about the monopoly powers of railways were much less pressing than the benefits for national unification and identity that could flow from a nationwide railway network. Belgian interests had sought permission to build a railway from Brussels to Antwerp before the country secured its independence, but their then Dutch rulers had rejected the idea.

One of the notable features of Belgium today is that it has the densest network of railways in the world, and the densest population in Europe (apart from the special case of the Principality of Monaco). In terms of population density, Holland runs Belgium close, but Belgium, slightly smaller in area, has almost three times the length of track miles (6,893 miles, compared with Holland's 2,313 miles).

Le Belge, the first Belgian-built locomotive.

The newly established Belgian government received (and rejected) a number of piecemeal private proposals to build individual lines, which alerted them to the potential for a properly planned railway network to rejuvenate the national economy. The government was fearful that a purely private-led initiative could be taken over and monopolised by large banks. So, before a single track was laid, the government drew up plans for a national network of railways. In 1834 plans were announced to build a railway between the industrial town of Mons and the port of Antwerp, via Brussels. The first stage of the line, between Brussels and Malines (Mechelen), was completed in 1835, to become the first steam passenger railway in mainland Europe.

It was once again powered by British steam; the service's first three locomotives were *L'Elephant*, built by Tayleur & Co. of the Vulcan Foundry, Warrington; and two Stephenson locomotives, *La Fleche* ('the arrow') and one actually named *Stephenson*. For the inaugural trip all three locomotives together pulled a train of thirty carriages, carrying about 1,000 passengers. *L'Elephant* managed the return journey single-handedly. A year later the next phase of the line, to Antwerp was opened. Further sections of railway were completed in the next few years so that, by 1843, the key parts of the national network, forming a roughly north–south/east–west cross were complete, linking Ghent and Ostend, the French and German borders, Courtrai and Namur.

The British influence continued; the Liege–Namur Railway was opened by a British company, and was due to be run by locomotives designed by Thomas Russell Crompton and built by Tulk and Ley of Whitehaven. However, the first batch was undelivered, due to the railway being incomplete, and they were eventually sold to the South Eastern Railway in England.

Subsequent development of the network was also heavily state-influenced. Many lines were privately funded, but they were built on a twenty-year lease, after which they would revert to public ownership. Many of them were operated by the state railway company. Within a decade of the first railway line opening, little Belgium had 350 miles (560km) of track, eighty stations, 143 locomotives and 25,000 items of rolling stock; rail-based international trade was booming and the port of Antwerp was one of the leaders in Europe.

Like much of Europe, Belgium was heavily influenced by the British railway model. It adopted the Stephenson gauge of 4ft 8½in, drove on the same left side of the tracks as Britain and its first home-built Locomotive – *Le Belge* – was another Robert Stephenson design, based on his Patentee class and built under licence by the British-born Belgian entrepreneur John Cockerill.

As we have seen, by 1843 Belgium had continuous tracks linking it to neighbouring countries. One of the fears of countries in nineteenth-century continental Europe – particularly countries with same-gauge tracks as their neighbours – was of the railways becoming a corridor for invasion. A dispute with France in the 1860s over attempts by French companies to buy up Belgian railway assets (something the King of Belgium quickly vetoed), nearly led to war, but the Franco–German war of 1870 intervened to cut any more local hostilities short.

France

France was a relatively slow starter in developing a railway network. It had short lines to serve mine workings in the early nineteenth century, but the decisive starting point was an important piece of legislation in 1842. Prior to this, however, in 1814 a French engineer, Pierre Michel Moisson Desroches, proposed to the Emperor Napoleon to build seven short railways radiating out from Paris, to facilitate short journeys within his empire.

In 1823 a Royal Decree was granted to the Saint Etienne and Andrézieux Railway to build a 21km standard-gauge line, from the coal and iron industry centre of St Etienne to Andrézieux, near to Lyon, the main town of the south of France. The line opened for goods traffic in 1827 and for passengers in 1835 (with it laying claim to be the first passenger service in mainland Europe). Its main goods cargo was coal, from the coalfields of St Etienne to the more navigable reaches of the River Loire for onward transhipment. France's leading locomotive designer of the period was Marc Seguin, who built locomotives for this route. They featured multi-tube boilers, on which Seguin held an 1828 French patent, and which were to be one of *Rocket*'s secrets of success at Rainhill. Less successful were a massive mechanical blower to do the job of a blastpipe and the use of vertical cylinders.

Despite this promising start, France failed to keep up with its neighbours and business rivals over the next decade, as it struggled to cope with the damage and turbulence of the Napoleonic Wars. A lack of industrialisation also worked against it. The country's limited iron-making capacity meant it had to buy its rails and other railway iron goods from England, at a high cost. Thirdly, the demand for a railway network was not quite as strong, since France was rather less urbanised and industrialised than some of its neighbours. There was also strong opposition to the change the coming of the railway would bring. For example, the Rouen Chamber of Commerce in 1832 opposed a proposed railway from Paris, on the grounds that it would damage agriculture and the traditional way of life and harm the business of canals and rivers (unlike some of its neighbours, France had invested heavily in waterborne transport).

The nature of French government also worked against the railways. Whilst some of its neighbouring states had quite strong central governments, France's democratic process involved lengthy debates in parliament. Railways were a topic that divided both the political class and the public at large. The nation's financial institutions and business sector were not strong enough to bring forward large railway schemes without government help. The opposition to railways knew this and brought pressure to bear on any potential paymasters in the public realm. The net result of all this was that only a few scattered railway schemes were built in 1830s France.

The big change came with a new piece of legislation in 1842. This steered a middle course between Britain's laissez-faire, free-market approach to railway building and the government-built and controlled system of somewhere such as Belgium. It meant that the French public purse carried out the necessary land purchase (often compulsorily), paid infrastructure costs such as bridges, tunnels, civil engineering and trackbed, and then left the private sector to fund the tracks, stations and rolling stock, and pay the operating costs, which were subject to rules laid down by government. For example, the government laid down a maximum annual dividend payable by the railway company and took a slice of any dividend in excess of it. It also ensured cut-price travel for anyone (or anything) on government business.

Initially, the private sector only leased the trackbed on a thirty-six-year lease (extended by Napoleon III to ninety-nine years). This paved the way for the eventual nationalisation of the railway network. This hybrid system of operating had its strengths. Government control meant that it avoided the worst of the duplication of British railway lines and the building of 'no hope' routes in times of railway mania. By the same token, France had need of certain stretches of railway that served important strategic military needs (such as along France's eastern border with Germany) but which would never have got built under a purely free-market system.

At the same time, the French network had its flaws. By 1855 the network was largely in the hands of six large companies, which formed spokes radiating out from Paris. These spokes served the centre well but cross-country movement was far more problematic. It is only a slight exaggeration to say that it was a case of lost passengers having to go back to Paris and starting again. The fatal weakness of this approach was highlighted during the Franco–Prussian war of 1870, when the German grid pattern of railway lines proved far more effective for military purposes.

Speaking of the impact of war, French railways, like so many others, followed British standards in terms of things such as gauge and the left-hand running of trains (not to mention buying most of the hardware from Britain). After the Franco–Prussian war, Alsace and Lorraine were annexed to become part of Germany. German railways drove on the right and, as part of their Germanification, the railways in those annexed areas were made to do the same. Despite being long since returned to France, Alsace and Lorraine still follow that practice, and a system of flyovers had to be introduced to link the region's railways with the rest of the national network. As far as earlier British influence is concerned, many of the earliest locomotives in France were British models. Stephenson's *Patentee* and long-boiler locomotives were built there under licence and a British locomotive manufacturing plant was set up at Sotteville to supply the French railways.

Colonial Railways: The Case of India

The British government decided early on that railways would be a good thing for the colonies. All other considerations aside, it would make a small colonial army infinitely more mobile in responding to disaffection among the native population. The former colony that first springs to mind in the context of railways is India, though most of its railway history tales place after our self-imposed cut-off point of 1830.

Ideas for a railway from Madras were floated as early as 1832. But this was condemned by both British and Indian interests as 'a premature and expensive undertaking and a hazardous and dangerous venture'. As grounds for their opposition they cited problems including poverty and dispersal of the population, making for low volumes of traffic, the country's extreme climate (violent rains, winds and a harsh sun), the difficult topography (mountains, deserts and dense forests), the unprotected nature of the countryside through which the railways would have to pass, and the difficulty and expense of recruiting competent and trustworthy engineers. The doubters would eventually be proved wrong about passenger volumes once the railways were built. In the first five years the level of passenger travel increased five-fold, from 535,000 to more than 2.4 million, and kept growing at that rate for the next five years.

As in Germany, the railways fostered a growing national identity as people from one state came into contact with others on their travels. But it also threw issues of class (or rather race and caste) into sharper and less positive relief.

But a new economic argument entered the debate in 1846, after the major failure of the American cotton crop left the British cotton industry frantically searching for alternative sources of supply. Parts of India were a possibility, but the lack of communications meant it would have taken an unacceptably long time for the crop to reach a seagoing port, for delivery to England. Lord Dalhousie was President of the Board of Trade, having been Vice President under William Gladstone, a track record that made him uniquely qualified among politicians to judge the merits of railway schemes. As it happens, he was made Governor General of India in 1847. He proposed a series of railways liking the ports of Bombay, Calcutta and Madras.

A bill to initiate the Great Indian Peninsular Railway Company (later known as the Peninsular) was put before Parliament in 1847, but was subsequently withdrawn at the insistence of the East India Company, who at that time ruled large parts of India, and it was not until the beginning of 1849 that the Company came into being. It offered free land and a guaranteed 5 per cent return on their investment for any British company willing to build railways in India.

At about the same time (1845) the East Indian Railway was founded to provide railways to northern and eastern India. It ordered eight loco-motives from the Vulcan foundry in Newton-le-Willows, Merseyside, and started laying track. The first stretch of line, from Bori Bunder (Mumbai) to Thane, was ready by November 1852. Officials took a test run on it that month but it was not until April 1853 that the official opening took place. Three locomotives – *Sindh*, *Sahib* and *Sultan* – pulled a fourteen-coach train with up to 400 passengers along the 34km route to Thane. The Governor declared the day a public holiday and the 400 passengers indulged in some lavish dining at the end of their forty-five-minute jour-ney.

Then there was the issue of the gauge of the new railways. Lord Dalhousie wanted a mid-point between standard and the Great Western broad gauge. He settled upon a gauge of 5ft 6in (1,675mm) and the gov-ernment agreed this in 1851. But the then Viceroy of India, Lord Mayo, was a great enthusiast of the metric system and promoted 3ft gauge (roughly 1m) railways wherever they were likely to have lighter traffic. He even tried to get the 5ft 6in lines converted to his quasi-metric stand-ard. The result was a long series of arguments, repeated whenever a new length of railway was proposed. By the mid-1800s India had four different 'standard' gauges.

The American Civil War meant further disruption to Britain's cotton supply and created an opportunity for India to increase its market share. One line, the Gaikwad Baroda State Railway, was so keen to get its new railway into use that it would not wait for the delivery of locomotives from England, but harnessed buffalo to pull its wagons. At this time the Indians had no locomotive-building capability of their own. The first Indian-built locomotive would not appear until 1895.

There was also a great dispute about the differential treatment of pas-sengers. Almost all European passengers travelled first class in near European-standard luxury, whilst Indian passengers were condemned to squalor in the overcrowded third- and later fourth-class carriages. There was even a long dispute about whether the company should provide the third-class carriages with toilets.

The funding of the railways also proved controversial. The Bengal–Nagpur railway was paid for by the Rothschild family, but the British government decided that their guaranteed interest on their investment should be paid for by a tax on the local peasantry. Thus the richest family in the world was being subsidised by some of the poorest. Mahatma Gandhi would later focus on the treatment of the Indian population by the railway companies as an argument for independence. Corruption also added to the burden on the Indian population. Railway companies were encouraged by the high and guaranteed rates of return to overspend wildly on their schemes. It was calculated that in the 1850s and '60s a mile of Indian railway cost an average of £18,000 to construct, against the dollar equivalent of £2,000 for an average mile of American track.

Finally, evidence later emerged of corruption, by both members of the British Indian government and by the firms that supplied the hardware for the railways, with the result that railway lines and other hardware cost nearly twice what it should have done. The extra cost was, of course, paid by the Indian population through taxes and ticket prices. There was also the building of 'white elephant' lines as a result of lobbying and sometimes bribery on the part of commercial interests who would benefit from them. The cost of these lines would again be borne by the Indian taxpayer and traveller.

On the positive side, the railways are credited by some with dramatically reducing the problem of famine caused by rainfall failures. However, others argue that an excessive focus on exporting goods to Britain would later stop the railways doing all that they could to prevent events such as the Great Bengal Famines of 1909 and 1942.

More generally, Wolmar concludes that the railways did not do all that they could have done to transform the Indian economy, as they did in many other countries. Had they treated their passengers as customers, rather than vassals, and used the economic power of the railways to their full potential to generate new skills and industries, some of the hostility towards the colonial powers might have been avoided.

Under independence Indian Railways have grown to be the world's eighth largest employer, with 1,308,000 employees; and the fourth largest rail network – 41,861 route miles or 67,368km. (March 2017 figures).

And the Rest of the Empire

Across much of the British Empire, railway building did not get under way until well after our end date of 1830, hence our relatively brief coverage of it.

The first railway in **Australia** was privately owned and operated, built in 1831, but it was only a colliery line, operating on an inclined plane as a gravitational railway. Serious railway building did not get under way until the 1850s. Perhaps the most striking thing about the Australian experience is the lack of coordination between the states (much of the early railway building initiatives took place at a state, rather than a federal, level). This is most evident in the choice of gauge. Despite urging from Britain to adopt a single gauge across the sub-continent, the states insisted upon going their own way, with the result that Australia now has three different gauges of railway – something that has caused it problems ever since wherever the different gauges met. One line – the Mount Gambier – is described as 'isolated by gauge and of no operational value'. Anyone seeking a case study of sustained bad decision-making need look no further.

Canada entered the railway-building age in the 1850s with two principal aims in mind; first to unite its far-flung provinces and second to maximise trade within Canada and minimise trade with the United States, so as to avoid becoming an economic satellite of America. Some more ambitious Canadians even hoped to rival or even surpass the United States economically. As one interpretation of this strategy, some entrepreneurs gave first priority to branches going into the United States (to supply their needs and stop them shopping elsewhere), secondly to Halifax Nova Scotia (as one end of a transatlantic link back to the mother country) and with links out to the rest of Canada itself being only third in importance.

Metropolitan rivalries between Montreal, Halifax and St John led to Canada building more railway lines per capita than any other industrialising nation. In particular, they overestimated the demand for transcontinental traffic, building three east–west lines – far more than the traffic could support. One after another the private companies operating them fell into debt and had to be bailed out by the government. Much of the freight they did carry was related to industries that already existed in Canada – wheat, coal-mining, timber and paper-making. Whilst these industries increased their markets, the railways did relatively little to promote new Canadian manufacturing more generally. Most of the manufactured goods the country needed continued to be imported from Great Britain and the United States.

The British built railways all across the Empire. Most colonies had something to export back to the home country – in addition to India's tea and Canada's wheat and timber, Malaya had its rubber, south America coffee and meat, and Australia and New Zealand meat products. In return, Britain would send them manufactured goods. Sometimes the outward-bound cargo could take on a human form, as the railways in areas such as southern Africa were used to open up the interior and encourage settlement (which would in time mean more custom for the railways). By far the grandest (and most imperialistic) example of this policy was Cecil Rhodes' unfulfilled plan for a Cape to Cairo railway, which would run the entire length of the continent without ever leaving British-controlled territory.

The British army would prevail upon local administrators across the Empire to build railways to meet strategic military needs, whether or not there was a civilian economic case for them. Where reasoned argument failed, they would sometimes be made to build them anyway. So in Sudan, the British army went into battle sedately, sailing down the Nile, but it built a railway (still in use) as it went, to supply it. This and subsequent hostilities would highlight the military importance – and the vulnerability – of the railways in wartime.

Sources

Unless otherwise stated, the illustrations for this book come from my own collection, the public realm or Wikipedia and Wikimedia Commons. Two Victorian and Edwardian publications I found particularly useful as sources of illustrations were Stretton's *The Development of the Locomotive* (1896) and Howden's *The Boys' Book of Locomotives* (1907) – details overleaf. (There must have been some well-informed Edwardian trainspotters!) Other sources are listed against the photographs.

Bibliography

Ayton, Richard and Daniell, William, *A Voyage Around Great Britain Undertaken in the year 1813* (Longmans, 1814).

Bogart, Dan, *The Turnpike Roads of England and Wales* (internet).

Bradley, Simon, *The Railways – Nation, Network and People* (Profile Books, 2015).

Burton, Anthony, *The Rainhill Story* (BBC Books, 1980).

Burton, Anthony, *Richard Trevithick: Giant of Steam* (Aurum, 2000).

Burton, Anthony, *The Canal Builders* (Pen and Sword, 2015).

Carlson, Robert E., *The Liverpool and Manchester Railway Project 1821–1831* (David & Charles, 1969).

Clarke, Stephen, *The Industrial Revolution: Why Britain Got There First* (2014).

Crump, Thomas, *The Age of Steam* (Robinson, 2007).

Darby, Michael, *Early Railway Prints* (HMSO, 1974).

Dendy Marshall, *Chapman Frederick – A History of Railway Locomotives until 1831* (Salzwasser Verlag, reprint of the 1928 volume).

Dow, Andrew, *The Railway – British Track since 1804* (Pen and Sword, 2014).

Evans, Eric J., *The Forging of the Modern State: Early Industrial Britain 1783–1870* (Longman, 1983).

Faith, Nicholas, *The World the Railways Made* (The Bodley Head, 1990).

Ferneyhough, Frank, *Liverpool and Manchester Railway 1830–1980* (Book Club Associates, 1980).

Fletcher, Malcolm and Taylor, John, *Railways: The Pioneer Years* (Studio Editions, 1990)

Garnett, A.F., *Steel Wheels* (Cannwood Press, 2005).

Guy, Andy and Rees, Jim, *Early Railways 1569–1830* (Shire, 2011).

Gwyn, David & Cossons, Neil, *Early Railways in England* (Historic England, 2017).

Hayes, Derek, *The First Railways* (an atlas) (The Times, 2017).

Howden, Joseph R., *The Boys' Book of Locomotives* (London, 1907).

Hylton, Stuart, *A History of Manchester* (Phillimore 2003, 2010).

Hylton, Stuart, *The Grand Experiment* (Ian Allan, 2007).

Hylton, Stuart, *What the Railways Did for Us* (Amberley, 2015).

James, Leslie, *A Chronology of the Construction of Britain's Railways 1778–1855* (Ian Allan, 1983).

Maggs, Colin, *Steam Trains* (Amberley, 2014).

Preece, Geoff, *Coal Mining* (City of Salford, 1981).

Ross, David, *The Steam Locomotive: A History* (Tempus, 2000).

Ross, David, *George and Robert Stephenson: A Passion for Success* (The History Press, 2010).

Simmons, Jack and Liddle, Gordon, *The Oxford Companion to British Railway History* (Oxford U.P., 1997).

Simmons, Jack, *The Victorian Railway* (Thames and Hudson, 1991).

Smith, Adam, *The Wealth of Nations* (first published 1776; Penguin edition, 1970).

Snell, J.B., *Early Railways* (Weidenfeld and Nicholson, 1964).

Stretton, Clement E., *The Development of the Locomotive* (Crosby Lockwood and Son, 1896).

Trevelyan, G.M., *Illustrated English Social History: 4* (Pelican Books, 1964).

Weightman, Gavin, *What the Industrial Revolution Did for Us* (BBC Books, 2003).

Wolmar, Christian, *Fire and Steam* (Atlantic, 2007).

Wolmar, Christian, *Railways and the Raj; How the Steam Age Changed India Forever* (Atlantic, 2017).

I have not attempted to list every internet source or online article I have referred to in the writing of this book – your own search engine should lead you to the great majority of them. But here at least are a few that may not be immediately obvious.

AnimatedEngines.com, Newcomen engine.

American-Rails.com, 1820s and 1830s Railroads – the Beginning.

Bogart, Dan, the turnpike roads of England and Wales.

Bogart, Dan and others, the development of the railway network in Britain 1825–1911.

British History, Entrepreneurs and Business Leaders – Joseph Sandars and other entries.

Citizendium, history of railways in the British Empire.

Coulls, Anthony, Railways as World Heritage Sites.

Daniel, John, the Great Western archive – blastpipes.

Engineering-timelines.com – Oystermouth Railway and other topics

French Railway Society.

The Gazette (official public record), The opening of the Liverpool and Manchester Railway 1830.

Grace's Guide, William Murdoch: Steam Engine.

Guardian Unlimited Home, track gauge.

Hilton, George W., A history of track gauge (2006).

History of the Great Western Railway, construction 1835–38.

The Industrial Railway Record, steam on the Penydarren tramway (April 1975).

SpellerWeb.net, John Speller's web pages.

Locomotives in profile, Pre-1825 locomotives

McGow, Peter, The Surrey Iron Railway (Wandle Industrial Museum, 2001).

Mike's Railway History.

Museum of American Heritage, Dreams of Steam

Notes and extracts on the history of the London and Birmingham Railway, the Train Now Standing.

www.parliament.uk, Roads and Railways: living heritage.

Preserved British Steam Locomotives, Invicta.

Quakers in the World, the Pease family.

SNCF.com, the story of French Rail.

Steam History Home, the Savery Pump.

Thoughtco, Railways; the workhorses of Empire and other subjects.
Victorian Web, Railways in British India.
US History.org, Early American Railroads.
Yorkshire Reporter, the History of the Middleton Railway.

Any errors or omissions that remain in the book, despite all this helpful guidance, are entirely my responsibility.

Index

Adler 202
Aeolipile 12
Agenoria 81
Agricola, Georgius 151
Allan, Thomas 50
America 191
American-type locomotives 198
Ar'ruf, Taqi 13
Australia 214

Beamish Museum 54
Belgium 206
Best Friend of Charleston 197
Bethell 148
Birkenshaw, John 146
Blackett, Christopher and
    others 55
Blastpipe 74, 78
Blenkinsop, John 43, 45, 48
Boiler explosions 47, 53, 70
Booth, Henry 90, 102
Boulton, Matthew and Watt 26, 30–1
Braithwaite, John 106
Branca, Giovanni 13
Brandling, Charles 116
Brandreth, Thomas Shaw 108
Brindley, James 142
British Empire 210, 214
Brunel, Isambard Kingdom 131, 158–9,
    165, 175

Brunel, Marc 159
Brunton, William and the mechanical
    traveller 51
Burstall, Timothy 106
Bury, Edward 87

Canada 214
Canals
    Aire and Calder Navigation 117
    Birmingham 136
    Blaenavon Navigation 135
    Bridgewater 136, 142, 178
    Caledonian 137
    Croydon 119–20
    Cromford 95
    Ellesmere 140
    Glamorganshire 36, 135
    Grand Junction 139, 147
    Huddersfield 138, 140
    Kennet and Avon 143
    Lancaster 140
    Leicester and Swannington 140
    Oakham 135
    Rochdale 136
    Somerset Coal Canal 95
    Stratford and Avon Canal 85–6
    Trent and Mersey 142
Carrolltan viaduct 192
Catch Me Who Can 41
Causey Arch 161

Chapman, William 146
China 151
Chittaprat/Royal George 71
Coalbrookdale 34, 196
Common carrier 195
Competition 169, 185
Corruption 213
Crawshay, Richard 36
Cubitt, William 139
Cugnot, Nicholas 28–30
Curr, John 148
Cyclopede 109

Darby, Abraham 145, 182
Darwin, Erasmus 28
Davis, Phineas 196
De Garay, Blasco 13
Delhousie, Lord 211
Democracy 171, 186
De Witt Clinton 197, 199
Diolkos 149
Disraeli, Benjamin 171
Dundas, Charlotte 15

Egypt 12
Elizabeth I 153
Ericsson, John 106
Eton College 171
European railways 170, 201
Evans, Oliver 28
Experiment 198

Fenton, Murray and Wood – engine
    builders 45
Finance 187
France 208

Gauge 154, 156
George III 127
Germany 201
Gladstone, William 168
Gray, Thomas 96
Greece 149

Hackworth, Timothy 48, 55, 72, 76, 83
Hedley, William 55
Hero 12

Hetton Colliery 50
Homfray, Samuel 36
Huskisson, William 91

India 210
Industrial Revolution
    and railways 181
Invicta 75

James, William 85, 130
Jeaffreson, John Cordy 167
Jessop, William 97, 139
John Bull 198

Kennedy, John 105
Killingworth Colliery 172
Kyan, John 147

La Fleche 206
Laing, Samuel 170
Lardner, Dionysius 131, 173
Le Belge 206
L'Elephant 206
Locke, Joseph 91
Locomotion 69, 71
Losh, William 65

Macadam, John 179
Middleton Colliery 43
Monopoly and competition 184
Multi-tube boiler 77, 103
Murdoch, William 27, 30–2

Navvies 140
Newcomen, Thomas 21, 23–4
Newton, Isaac 12–13
Novelty 103

Outram, Benjamin 95, 139
Overseas railways 191
Overton, George 37, 126

Papin, Denis 14, 19, 28
Parliament and Parliamentary processes 65,
    138, 163, 186
Patentee 202
Patents 65

Pease, Edward 93
Penydarren 37
Peto, Samuel 141
Phoenix 197
Planet 110
Platerails and plateways 148
Police – railway and others 104
Pollution 172
Pontcysyllte Viaduct 140
Puffing Billy and *Wylam Dilly* 55, 57, 87

Rack-and-pinion railway 43
Railway mania 137
Rail journey – first 36
Railways:
    Baltimore and Ohio 193
    Camden and Amboy 193, 200
    Canterbury and Whitstable 129
    Carmarthenshire Railway 118
    Delaware and Hudson 195
    Grand Junction 91, 96
    Granite Railway 195
    Kilmarnock and Troon 67, 97
    Lake Lock Rail Road 117
    Leicester and Swannington 88
    Liverpool and Manchester 67, 96, 148
    London and Brighton 94, 121
    London and Birmingham 88, 147
    London, Chatham and Dover 131
    Mohawk and Hudson 198
    Newcastle and Carlisle 98, 123, 125
    New Jersey Railroad 192
    Oystermouth 122
    Sirhowy tramway 118
    Stockton and Darlington 69, 148
    Stratford and Moreton 71, 174
    Surrey Iron Railway 118–19
    Warrington and Newton 113
    West Coast Main Line 92
Rainhill 99
Ramsbottom, John 48
Rastrick, John 79, 86
Red Flag Act 180
Regulation of Railways Act 1844 168
Rennie, John 69, 139
Road journey times 178
Road travel improvements 118

Rocket 102
Romans 134, 150, 157
Roosevelt, Nicholas 192
Rothschild family 213

Safety valves 47
Sandars, Joseph 96
Sans Pareil 76, 84
Savery, Thomas 15
Saxonia 203
Seguin, Marc 90, 103
Shaftesbury, Earl of 168
Smith, Adam 182
South Carolina Canal and Railroad
    108, 196
Standedge tunnel 140
Steam Elephant 54
Steam locomotion – dangers of 172
Stephenson, George 45, 50, 55, 61, 66, 98,
    156, 166, 175
Stephenson Junior, Robert 75, 91, 100,
    144, 196
Stephenson Senior, Robert 50, 62
Stevens, John 195, 200
Stevens, Robert 200
Stourbridge Lion 79
Summit Hill Railroad 194
Symington, William 15, 28

Tanfield Waggonway 161
Telford, Thomas 179
Time and timekeeping 185
Tom Thumb 195
Trevithick, Richard 13, 32–42, 47
Turnpike 178
Tyler Hill and tunnel 131

Urbanisation 182

Verbiest, Ferdinand 15
Vignoles, Charles 91, 94
Vital statistics:
    Brunton's mechanical traveller 53
    Invicta 76
    Locomotion 73
    Penydarren locomotive 39
    Puffing Billy 59

Prince Regent 45
  Rocket 104
  Royal George 75
  Sans Pareil 78
  Steam Elephant 55
  Stourbridge Lion 82
  Wylam locomotive 40
Vitruvius 12
Vivian, Andrew 32

Walker, James 100
Watt, James 24–5
Wealth of Nations and division of
  labour 182
Wellington, Duke of 110, 171
Wilkinson, John 27
William I (King of Prussia) 202
Wood, Nicholas 97, 134, 175
Wylam Colliery 55
Wylam locomotives 55

The History Press

The destination for history
www.thehistorypress.co.uk